YOUR DREAMS AND MAKING THEM WORK FOR YOU

WORKBOOK

JOE FRIEDMAN

CARROLL & BROWN PUBLISHERS LIMITED

First published in 2007 in the United Kingdom by

Carroll & Brown Publishers Limited
20 Lonsdale Road
London NW6 6RD

Designer Emily Cook
Illustrator Rupert Soskin

Text © Joe Friedman, 2007
Illustrations and compilation
© Carroll & Brown Limited, 2007

ISBN-10: 1-904760-26-0
ISBN-13: 978-1-904760-26-9

10987654321

Reproduced by RALI in Spain
Printed and bound in Spain by Vivapress

Contents

Introduction

This aim of this book is to show you through experience just how joyful, creative, wise, useful and entertaining dreams are. It is full of practical exercises to help you understand and use your dreams to solve problems and gain insight. You will learn to value your dreams – not because Freud or someone else has said they are beneficial – but because you've discovered it for yourself. Through all this, you may find why the original meanings of the word dream were "joy", and "shout of joy".

At first glance, dreams can seem like a wild garden – unruly and chaotic. Our dreams contain beautiful flowers, useful plants and unexpected vistas – but all this is hidden from us. Fortunately dreams, unlike gardens, respond quickly to our attention and start to reward it. The first chapter, "Getting Started with Dreams", gives the information and tools needed to begin to reap this rich harvest.

Become your Own Authority
The fact that dreams seem so chaotic and confused has fostered the growth of the dream "expert" and the dream dictionary. Dream of a tree and you are told your life will bear

unexpected fruit. Nonsense. Dream images are specific to your life and experience. No one dreams of a generic tree: rather it's the tree under which you buried your first dog or the tree which hid your first kiss from your parents. Here, you'll learn simple techniques to help you discover why *you* dreamed of Tony Soprano, a war-torn old cat or a dangerously speeding car.

The theories of the dream "greats" – Freud, Jung, etc. – can help you get to grips with your dreams. Chapter 4, "What We Can Learn From…" is full of practical exercises to enable you to apply their important insights.

Being a dream authority doesn't mean you have to work solo: it's a joy to share dreams with others, getting their feedback and having your understanding enriched by new and different perspectives. Chapter 7, "Sharing Dreams", gives advice on finding a dream partner or starting your own dream group. You'll also learn about the extraordinary phenomena such sharing produces.

Peak Creativity

Scientific research shows us dreams are a time of peak creativity. Our brains are as active as when we're awake and the chemicals that enable us to make unusual connections are at their maximum. Einstein's theory of relativity was inspired by a dream, as was Mary Shelley's *Frankenstein*, Paul McCartney's "Yesterday", several Nobel Prize-winning discoveries and many world-changing inventions.

You can use your natural dream creativity to solve problems in your daily life. Need help with a relationship that is stuck? Preparing a homework assignment or presentation? Can't see your way forward at work? Need advice on getting around a neighbour from hell? All these everyday problems can be solved in your dreams, and this book shows you how, with step-by-step instructions.

Rose Coloured Glasses

Whether we wear rose-coloured glasses or see the world through a glass darkly, we all experience the world differently. For some of us, our daily world is filled with positive possibilities, for others, potential disaster.

However we see the world, we find justification for it in our experience. If we feel that people respect us, we find others treat us with dignity. If we fear attack, we interpret all kinds of ordinary behaviour as a threat. Because of this, it's difficult for us to truly see the "lenses" that colour our every experience.

Our dreams can show us these glasses. Bill, for example, had been taught that everyone is always looking after number one. That's how he behaved. He saw others doing the same. After he started working with his dreams, he began to wonder why everyone in his dreams was self-serving and selfish. Okay, that's how the world is… But why didn't he ever *dream* of anyone who

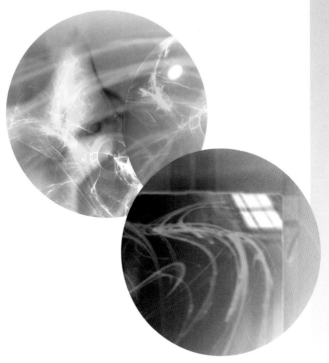

was friendly, helpful or loving? Bill began to question the way he thought "things are". He realized that what he was experiencing in his dreams was the way he constructed the world. Once he saw this, his dreams started to give him new experiences; they began to show him a new way of being.

This way of understanding dreams has enormous power – we can literally see our world-construction software in action, those "lenses" that make people and the world appear to us in the way they do.

The Value of Dreams

Most of us in the West start from the perspective that every experience must be made to "work" for us, must prove its "cash value". We feel that our time is precious and that anything we do must produce some tangible gain. One of the most damning criticisms of dreams is that they're meaningless garbage produced by the brain at night.

Recent scientific discoveries do *not* support this criticism. Nor does my experience and that of countless others. More to the point, if you do the exercises in this book you will find that your dreams earn their keep many times over.

Dreams have also helped me and others bring into question the work ethic that makes us feel we must profit from every moment of our lives. Many dreams are poetic and personal works of art. Once we start remembering our dreams, it is impossible not to appreciate the images, narratives, characters and the incredible cinema they create for us night after night.

Dreams also bring us into contact with something larger than ourselves: God, Spirit, Being, our higher Selves, the Unconscious, whatever you choose to call it. We are so much more than our limited perception of ourselves. At night, we can have an experience of a different realm of being.

How to Use this Workbook

My emphasis is on the practical: on giving you hands-on, or dreams-on, experience. Every chapter contains exercises you can do to deepen your understanding.

To get the most out of this book, I suggest you take an experimental approach. Try the exercises and see what happens. Learn from your own experience as well as mine.

Each chapter is complete in itself. For beginners, it's probably best to start at the beginning and work your way through the book. If you are more experienced, you can skip from topic to topic, following your desire. If you are interested in finding out how to control your dreams, go to "Lucid Dreaming"; if you're keen to develop your sixth sense check out "Dreaming through Space and Time".

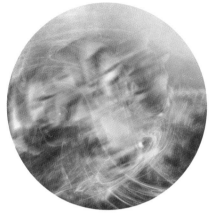

There is one proviso – you'll get the most out of this book if you're actively remembering and recording dreams as you read it. So, if you're not already keeping a dream diary, begin with the chapter "Getting Started with Dreams".

Learn by Doing

The best way to learn is by experience. Don't just read the chapters. Do the exercises in them. Part of what you'll discover is that dreams are incredibly responsive to what you want from them. Dreams are *idioplastic* – shaped by your ideas and desires. So whether you want to have lucid dreams, solution dreams, psychic dreams, Freudian dreams, Jungian dreams or all of these in succession, they will do their best to help. Go on, give them a chance. You won't regret it.

1

Getting Started
with Dreams

How to Remember Dreams

We all dream four or five times a night. The first dream – 15 minutes long – generally occurs a little more than an hour after we go to sleep. The last dream, which may last up to an hour, finishes around half an hour before we awake. In between are two or three dreams of increasing lengths.

The chart on the opposite page shows our sleep pattern. We'll talk more about this in the chapter on the physiology of dreams, but for now, we want to concentrate on what studies have shown us about remembering dreams. There are three main keys to this process.

First, you need to awaken during a dream. In the lab, when people are awoken during the REM cycle, 80 percent of the time they remember a vivid sensory experience. If, however, they are awoken one minute after the end of the REM cycle, most people remember little or nothing of the dream they would have remembered vividly a minute earlier.

At first thought, this seems a tall order. Wake up during a dream in the middle of the night while I'm asleep? Is this possible? A study by Rosalind Cartwright tested exactly this. She took 10 adults

When you wake up with a dream or dream image fresh in your mind, don't move.

into a dream laboratory and gave them instructions to try to make a fist when they realized they were dreaming. On seeing the fist, she would wake them up and record their dreams. All 10 adults were able to do this at least once during their first night in the laboratory. Most waited until the end of the REM period, so they "could find out what happened". Strangely, several had no awareness of making a fist.

Don't Move

What happens at the end of the dream that restricts dream recall? You turn over, move your arm, or otherwise perform what lab scientists call a "gross bodily movement". After this movement, most of your memory of the dream has gone.

This leads to the second key to dream recall. When you wake up with a dream or dream image fresh in your mind, *don't move*. Before you do anything, gather all the images and scenes you can remember and put them into words in your head. Some people find it helpful to give a dream a title. Don't move to write down the dream until you have it clear in your mind. Then do the minimum to record it. That means you have to have your tools

for recording the dream right by your bed. Every moment you spend searching for a pen or piece of paper will mean you lose some of your dream. For the same reason, write the dream down before you go to the toilet or rush for your cup of coffee.

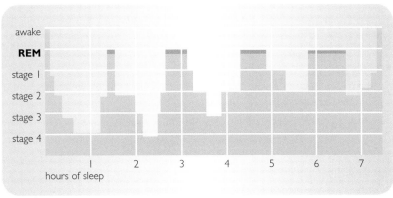

Dream recall is very fleeting. It is very state-specific; that is, once you are awake and start your daily activity, dreams retreat swiftly. It's true many of us have the experience of part of a dream coming back to us while showering, for example, or at some other time of the day, when something jogs our memory. This does happen, but considering you dream four or five times a night, every night, it's very rare. The best way to recall dreams is during the night, immediately after you've awoken with a dream fresh in your mind.

Record It

The final key to remembering a dream is to record it immediately. Doing this means you capture most of the details and feelings of the dream. These details and feelings will be crucial for the rest of the exercises in this book. They are what make your dream uniquely yours. Lots of people may dream about falling, being naked in a public place, or being chased by shadowy figures. No one will dream about these things in exactly the same way as you. The detail in your dream is the key to how you uniquely see the world. Recording it right away ensures you don't lose this detail.

If you recall only an image or a short fragment, or something, which in the middle of the night seems trivial, record it anyway. We're not best able to judge the relevance of our dreams in the middle of the night.

You can record a dream by writing it down or speaking into a voice recorder. If you do the latter, you'll need to transcribe the dream the following

day – otherwise you won't be able to make sense of the detail in the recording. In any case, you may be a bit freaked by the sound of your voice immediately after you've awoken from a dream. You will definitely sound other-worldly. (In fact, this is a good exercise just to get a sense of how different a space you occupy while dreaming.)

I save time during the night by writing down notes about my dream on a pad of paper, and then transcribing them more fully into my dream diary. If you take this path, make sure your notes are extensive enough to bring the whole dream back. And don't procrastinate about transcribing it – do it in the next 24 hours.

Generally, it is best to record a dream as it happened, in chronological order. There are two exceptions to this. Record any unusual expressions or names and made-up words first. These examples of dream work often go quickly, and if you wait to record them until the appropriate point in the dream, you may lose them or find yourself doubting the word and making up more "sensible" alternatives. Similarly, record any dialogue you remember verbatim immediately. We don't often

The detail in your dream is the key to how you uniquely see the world.

remember the exact words people speak in a dream, just the sense of them, but if we do remember the exact words, they can provide us with a link to our daily life.

The Three Keys

These are the three keys to dream recall. Wake during a dream, gather the dream up and put it into words before moving, and then, record it immediately. Ideally you record your dream in your dream diary (see opposite page).

Tools of the Trade

If you sleep by yourself, you have a much wider range of options for recording your dreams. You can use a voice-operated tape recorder or digital recorder – the latter is really ideal for this. Or you can use the classic pen and paper. But make sure you can get hold of either with the minimum of movement.

If you have a partner sleeping by you, things become more complicated. You don't want to ruin your day life by waking him or her repeatedly in the night! Perhaps the most important tool of the trade here is conversation. Include your partner in your dream project. Tell him or her what you are up to, and if your partner is interested, share your dreams with him or her.

With a partner, a tape recorder is probably out, and you'll be restricted to pen and paper. I've taped a tiny flashlight to a pen and keep a thick magazine by my bed with a fresh sheet of paper on it. When I wake with a dream, I grab the magazine and write on the side of the bed, shielding my partner from the light of my flashlight/pen. If you have a partner who sleeps lightly, it's sometimes more politic to go to the bathroom (where you should keep a separate pen and paper) to write down your dream. This obviously involves more movement and potentially less dream recall, but it may be worth the sacrifice to keep a happy home.

Add Desire

You need to add one more ingredient to remember dreams regularly – the desire to remember your dreams. Apart from the technical knowledge on how to remember them – the three keys – the crucial factor in dream recall is wanting to do so. Since you've bought this book, you clearly have the desire to remember and explore your dreams. Let's harness this desire.

As you fall asleep, repeat to yourself "I want to remember a dream tonight. I can and will awake with a vivid dream fresh in my mind." If this form of words feels awkward, you might feel happier asking or praying for a dream. "Please may I recall a vivid dream tonight," or "I pray that I remember a vivid dream tonight." Bear in mind, however you ask for a dream, it needs to feel comfortable for you. Remember the three keys – you need to awaken during a dream, don't move until the dream is clear in your mind, and record it immediately. Finally, go to sleep with your request for a dream fresh in your mind.

FOR HARD NUTS ONLY

The above will work for the vast majority of people. But for some, more radical measures may be needed. The following ideas are only for those who have tried the above for a couple of weeks without success.

- Get a friend who goes to bed later than you to call you about 70 minutes after you go to sleep.
- Drink a litre of water before you go to bed. When you wake up needing to go to the toilet, don't move. Search your mind for a fragment of a dream. Reel in the rest of the dream. Write it down. Now go to the toilet.

And only for the seriously hard nuts:

- Set your alarm (on its lowest volume) every hour through the whole night. One alarm will undoubtedly go off during a dream.

Keeping a Dream Diary

Like a person, your dreams like to be appreciated. You've started the process by buying this book and starting to remember your dreams. Your dreams may have already responded. Perhaps you've had some especially vivid or interesting dreams since buying the book. A dream may even have helped you decide on its purchase.

But while your dreams, like people, will respond to an initial interest, a more substantial relationship requires them being given a special place in your life. Think of yourself as a dream. If you'd responded to someone's call by coming to visit them and half the time he or she didn't pay you any attention and the other half you found yourself written on scraps of paper littered around his or her bed, how would you feel?

If your dreams come by and get no response, again like people, they withdraw. (Fortunately, unlike people, dreams are very forgiving, so a slight can easily be overcome.) Probably the best way to make dreams feel you want to develop a relationship with them is to buy a dream journal or diary, a special book where they'll have a place to grow and develop.

Different people have different ideas of what a dream diary should be. Some dream diaries are works of art, as intricately illustrated as any medieval illuminated manuscript. Some are simple writer's pads. Some people prefer loose-leaf diaries, others prefer hardcover volumes, which form satisfying stacks on a prominent book shelf.

Some people type their dreams into a computer folder and a computer dream diary has some real advantages. With the various desktop search mechanisms – e.g. Google Desktop Search – you can search your dream diary for a title, character's name, or a scene of action, in a moment. Lately, I've taken to having both a computer dream diary, for the search possibilities it offers, and a printed one, so I can draw pictures and browse through it. The form of diary you choose should appeal to your dreams, so try to get a sense of what they'd like. Perhaps you could even ask for a dream to tell you.

Whatever the physical form of your dream journal, try to include the key elements listed on the following pages for every dream you record.

Have Fun

If all this sounds a bit like hard work, that's enormously misleading. Keeping a dream diary can be great fun. It can be an outlet for all the creative energies you don't get a chance to exercise in your everyday life.

Keeping a dream diary can be great fun. It can be an outlet for all the creative energies you don't get a chance to exercise in your everyday life.

It's probably been years since you've kept any kind of diary. You may have been inhibited by feeling you didn't have enough artistic or verbal ability, or that the stories you had to tell were painful or not very interesting.

The advantage of keeping a dream diary is that you're dealing with a powerful, natural source of creativity. No matter how hopeless you are at telling stories or jokes during the day, at night your natural storytelling ability is unleashed. No matter how unchallenging your day life, at night you're having incredible adventures. In the day, you may feel stuck in a role – you're a parent, a teacher or an accountant. At night, you play many different parts

THE KEY ELEMENTS IN YOUR DREAMS

A title If you have a paper diary, the title of your dream will be your search mechanism; when you're scanning through your diary looking for a particular dream, the title is what you'll look for. Make it stand out literally – by using different coloured ink or capital letters – and figuratively – by making the title memorable. Not "A Dream About a Fish", but rather "The Shark That Ate My Knee". Plays on words, vivid imagery and vulgar expressions can all make a title memorable. After you've kept your diary for a week, go back over it and see if you can remember your titles. If not, try to be more outrageous. As I said earlier about remembering a dream, formulating a title (while you're lying with your eyes closed and before moving) can help enormously in preserving the dream until you write it down. While this preliminary title serves as an *aide-mémoire*, you may find it useful to formulate another, more striking, title as part of your search mechanism.

Date/Time It doesn't matter whether you date your dreams for the day after you've dreamed them or the night before, but whatever you decide to do, stay consistent. If you have several dreams a night, try to note the times, too.

Dream content Write down the dream in as much detail as you can. Include everything you remember (the colour of the car, the kind of dog, what was said and how, etc.). Record anything that strikes you as unusual, incongruous, strange. Even in dreams that feel very mundane, there is often an element that stands out and can make us think. Pay special attention to these elements. I've spoken about noting down any unique speech, verbal expressions, or unusual names immediately you awaken. If you're writing your dream directly into your journal, record these first. Such verbal expressions tend to fade quickly and be subject to doubt – "was his name Geoff? Or was it Gerald?" Don't limit yourself to recording the dream in words. Pictures, drawings, cartoons and sketches can bring a dream to life. Sometimes a verbal description of a scene doesn't adequately convey the significance of the positioning of the characters or the arrangement of the room. A simple drawing can do this in a moment. If you have a Busby Berkeley moment while dreaming and find yourself looking down at choreographed movement, draw it. Images like this can be in the form of mandalas or other archetypes. Often, they provide the key to understanding a dream and grasping its meaning. If you don't do the sketch, you won't make the connection. Don't be limited by some idea of your (inadequate) artistic ability. These drawings are for you! Some people have found drawing in their dream journal was the start of a talent they never knew they had.

Day residue If anything in your dream reminds you immediately of something that happened the previous day(s), note it here.

Life The power of working with dreams comes from the way they connect with, and comment on, your day world.

in many different dramas. Keeping a dream diary is a powerful way of tapping into your alter-egos, all of whom embody your natural potentialities.

You can't make the connections if you don't have both the dream and the day events present in the same place. Write a couple of sentences about what's going on in your life and/or the issues with which you're engaged. Some people like to do this before they go to bed, thus setting a context for the dreams they then have. This is a good way of focusing your mind, and something you should try on the nights you're attempting to recall a dream.

I kept my first dream diary for more than a year without writing down anything about what was going on in my life. I thought I'd remember. I didn't. I thought the dreams would remind me what was happening. They don't. Years later, I can't make any sense of the dreams from this diary. I can't even recall the sense they made at the time. Don't make the same mistake. The best way to avoid it is to treat the dream diary as a mini-journal for what is going on in the day.

Associations (optional) Of what do the various details of your dream remind you? (More on this in Chapter 4, What We Can Learn From ... Freud.)

Analysis Often, if you're keeping a regular dream diary, you'll leave a space for the analysis. I'll be showing you many different ways of working with dreams in the coming pages. Leave space after your dreams for this, and for further thoughts.

SAMPLE DREAM DIARY

Title: Dream House

Date: March 2, 2005

Dream: We'd moved into a beautiful house by the sea. We'd bought it with another couple. It was absolutely gorgeous – lots of glass facing the open sea, open plan for the most part, though toward the back there were some rooms which, while open, were more secluded. There was a chair facing the back from which you could see a beautiful babbling river. I sat there and let the beauty wash over me.

The house was situated near an inlet, with another house and landing on the other side.

There were some problems. The main door slammed and Sheila thought it would be worse when there was a southwest wind. She wanted the door moved.

I was really just thrilled to be there. I said to Sheila, "I never thought I'd live in such a lovely place."

Day Residue: Met Sarah who said she was planning to move.

Life: I'm about to move to a new job in the same company. It's my dream job. I've been trying to restrain my excitement about it, just in case I'm disappointed.

Associations: Holiday by the sea, open feeling of air and sea. Great freedom.

Analysis: The dream won't let me pretend I'm not excited. It links the job, which I've worked hard for, with having a great view and freedom. The southwest wind makes me think of my new deputy, whose office is southwest of mine. Perhaps I'll need to watch him – he wanted the job but didn't get it.

Improving Dream Recall

The number of dreams you recall is very much a matter of choice. Often it makes sense to recall just as many dreams as you'll have time to get to grips with. Dream recall isn't an Olympic sport. More is not necessarily better.

CATEGORIES OF DREAM RECALL

I've broken down the extent of dream recall into seven categories, for use in the accompanying chart.

No dream recall
(perhaps the only absolutely clear one)

Sense This is a feeling of having dreamed, but you're left with no content.

Image This is where you remember a visual image, mood, song or thought.

Fragment Tick this if your image is more like a scene – with action, movement, flow.

Partial You tick this when you recall several scenes with some kind of link between them, but still have a sense of having forgotten most of the dream.

Majority If you feel you've recalled most of the dream, but have a sense of having missed a bit in the beginning or middle, this is the box to tick.

Whole dream This is only for those occasions when you have no sense of having forgotten anything significant.

The last thing you want is to feel you have to recall every dream, every night, and end up exhausted with piles of dreams you need to transcribe and don't know what to do with. So when I talk about improving dream recall I am not talking about quantity, but quality. We will see later that whatever you recall – even the smallest fragment, image or mood – can be helpful and useful. But even given that, there is often a sense of loss when you wake up with just an awareness of having dreamed, or remembering just an isolated image of what you vaguely recall was an epic tale.

CREATING A DREAM RECALL CHART

First of all, you don't want to be filling out a chart in the middle of the night. So, when you record a dream in the night, make a brief notation on how good your recall was. Do the chart in the morning.

Under the date, always include the days you make a conscious attempt to remember a dream, whether you end up remembering one or not. Also, include days you remember any part of a dream without any specific intention to do so. Don't include every day of the week. What we're trying to achieve here is better recall on the days when you attempt to remember dreams.

Write down the time you woke up with a dream. If you remember more than one dream a night, include each dream as a separate line, distinguishing them by the time you've recalled them.

Tick the appropriate category column (see box) and, under Notes, record anything you think significant. You can alter the chart to suit your own needs.

Our aim is for you to remember more of the dreams you do recall in more detail, more vividly.

Using a Chart

A dream recall chart can help you achieve this. Below is an example to copy plus a sample filled-out version. Your aim in keeping the chart is to move your ticks higher and higher up the recall spectrum (see box) on the days you try to recall dreams. Ideally, you'd like most of your ticks to be in the Majority or Whole boxes. Keep the chart until you have at least seven days of ticks. You may already notice an improvement in dream recall. Whether you do or not, try to review each one in your mind or on paper. You're trying to capture the external and internal factors that were at play.

Obvious external factors that might diminish dream recall are if you are exhausted, ill, have eaten too much or are inebriated. Maybe there is a fluctuation with medications you take or perhaps the factors are more subtle. It may be that particular foods, drinks or activities before going to sleep are inhibiting, like having a chat with your partner rather than reading a book or the paper, or working up until you go to bed, or watching television. Also think about your awakenings during the night – what happened immediately when you awoke? Did you jump up to go to the toilet or did you wake because you heard your baby crying?

Internal factors can be more subtle. Were you feeling positive or negative on going to bed? If positive, about what? If negative, how so? When you awoke what was your mood? Did any of this affect your recall?

Sometimes something obvious jumps out at you when you do this exercise. Other times it takes a bit more effort. But the reward should be immediate; you'll have a much more powerful sense of the amazing worlds you create and inhabit at night.

Date	Time of night	No dream	Sense of having a dream	Image	Fragment	Partial	Majority	Whole	Notes
Jan 5	3am		X						Very full from dinner, went to toilet
	7.10am				X				Alarm woke me
Jan 9	7am					X			Felt very low before going to bed
Jan 14	2.15am			X					
	6.55am						X		Just before alarm

Date	Time of night	No dream	Sense of having a dream	Image	Fragment	Partial	Majority	Whole	Notes

Improving Your Dream Senses

Most of us inhabit our dream world in a kind of fog. We are involved in what's happening, but only occasionally are struck by a sight, smell, sound, taste or touch. Mostly our movement is mechanical – we move in response to what's happening in the dream, without particular awareness of the stretching of our muscles or the grace and incredible complexity of our bodies.

When you think about it, none of this is very different from the way we inhabit the world while awake. How often do you smell flowers or hear birds on your way to work in the morning? How often do you notice a new shrub in someone's garden, or a new curtain in somebody's window? Often, when you do, you realize it's been there for weeks.

Improving your waking and dreaming senses often go hand in hand. Both simply require attention – and waking up from the fog of mechanical behaviour and assumption when awake, and when asleep. The exercise here can be practiced both in relation to dreaming and waking. In my experience, doing it in one realm improves your awareness of your senses in the other.

The point of these exercises is not just to sharpen your senses. You'll also learn how responsive your dreams are to your attention and requests. Later in the book, this will pay large dividends when we concentrate on developing your dream creativity, psychic abilities and capacity to have lucid dreams.

Sight and sound are the most common senses of which most of us are aware during dreams. Smell, taste and touch seem to be present in diminishing order. While we may be aware of motion, rarely are we aware of the pleasure and grace of movement in

KEEPING AN AWARENESS OF DREAM SENSES CHART

Keep a chart like the sample, below, for seven days of dreams. Then look at it to see what senses you are aware of in dreams, and to what extent. Use the scale of 0-6: 0 represents no awareness of smell, for example; 6 would be a smell that knocks your socks off (whether positively or negatively). Remember, we're looking at intensity here. Write down a number for all your senses, and also the awareness and pleasure you take in movement. Again, 0 would be no awareness of movement, and 6 would be an ecstatic state of inhabiting and appreciating your body. Experiences of 6 may be rare, but once you have them, you'll want to repeat them.

Date	Time	Extent of Dream Recall S/I/F/P/M/W	Sight	Smell	Hearing	Taste	Touch	Movement	Notes
Feb 10	6.30am	P	3	0	2	0	I	2	I heard people speaking, but not aware of the words
Feb 12	7.05 am	M	3	5	2	I	0	3	His breath smelt so bad I could taste it!
Feb 15	2.00 am	P	3	I	5	0	5	5	The stranger touched me, I jumped out of my skin
	7.00 am	F	2	0	2	I	2	I	Eating pizza but couldn't taste what kind

a dream – our own, or of others. Of course, body workers tend to be much more aware of movement in dreams, as are musicians of sound, and visual artists of sight. This parallels their waking acuity. But all of us could attain a much more acute awareness of our "weaker" senses.

Increasing Your Sensitivity

After a week, look at your results. Pick a sense that gets mostly 0s and 1s. Your aim is to increase the intensity of your dream (and waking) senses, and to expand your sensory repertoire. The way to do this is to pick a sense, say taste, and try to be especially aware of it during the day. Savour your food during meal times. Stop occasionally to think about and put into words what you're tasting. Be aware of the taste of your drink at night, your toothpaste, your partner's goodnight kiss. Taste something exquisite before going up to bed. Keep pulling yourself back to the taste, without getting distracted by the newspaper, tidying up, etc.

Then, just before going to bed, remind yourself you want to have a vivid sense of taste in your dreams. Do this on a regular basis until the intensity

of your experience of taste begins to move up the scale in your dreams. You will be amazed at how wonderful things can taste in dreams, especially foods that you hardly taste at all when awake. Repeat the same for the senses that are underplayed in your dream. Try to move your averages up the scale. Not everyone will be able to get all their senses towards the high end, but whatever improvement you manage, you'll find it will increase your desire to go to bed and dream.

Before going to bed, remind yourself you want to have a vivid sense of taste in your dreams.

Date	Time	Extent of Dream Recall	Sight	Smell	Hearing	Taste	Touch	Movement	Notes

Dreams and
the Body

Fascinating Discoveries from Scientific Research

After the discovery of Rapid Eye Movement (REM) in the 1950s, most scientists thought that dreaming and REM were one and the same thing. This had important implications because REM is controlled by a very primitive section of the brain, the pons, present in all mammals. Scientists who felt dreams had no meaning could argue that dreaming was a function of simple brain activation, effectively just random brain activity.

Recent research has made clear that REM is not necessary for human dreaming, and that dreaming is actually co-related with sections of the brain that are associated with reasoning, learning and memory. This research provides scientific support for seeing dreams as both meaningful and times of peak creativity.

The Discovery of REM

The modern story of dream research started just over 50 years ago. At the time, the common understanding of sleep was that it was when your brain and body shut down and recovered from the stresses of the day. Eugene Aserinsky, a graduate

student at the University of Chicago, had obtained an ancient EEG machine and, during several successive nights, had hooked up his eight-year-old son, Armond, to it. He put the electrodes on Armond's head, some of them close to his eyes. The EEG kept registering periods of intense activity, and Aserinsky assumed it was broken. The eye electrodes also registered movement. After several attempts at fixing the machine, Aserinsky stayed up one night to watch his son as he slept. Soon after his son fell asleep, he realized the EEG machine had started registering increased brain activity – and he could actually see his son's eyes moving under his eyelids. (Try watching your children's eyes as they sleep; you won't have long to wait. Children start REM very soon after they fall asleep. You'd have to wait quite a while to see an adult's eyes move.)

Aserinsky took his findings to his supervisor, Nathaniel Kleitman, who ran a sleep laboratory at the university. Neither was sure whether this was a genuine discovery, or a graduate student with a wonky EEG machine. To find out, they started

This is a coloured screen wave output from a polysomnigram of a sleeping subject. The top blue line represents an electroencephalogram (EEG) wave and the green trace at bottom corresponds to rapid eye movements. The changes observed using an EEG in normal sleep are often more dramatic than those relating to disease conditions.

bringing adults into the laboratory and recorded their EEG and eye movements throughout the night. They found that the adults had regular periods of rapid eye movement, which accompanied a very different EEG pattern than that of normal sleep. They started waking people during REM and N(on)REM periods. Eighty percent of the adults awoken during REM sleep remembered a dream, as against only 10 percent of those awoken during NREM periods.

For several years, Kleitman's and Aserinsky's discovery was mainly followed up only by a single researcher in Kleitman's laboratory, William Dement. Kleitman and Dement divided sleep into four discrete stages, and discovered that most people had a regular sleep pattern (see chart, page 13). Dement discovered REM sleep occurs in 90-minute cycles and that everyone has four to seven such REM periods a night. Each successive REM period is longer, and the longest is the one before you awake in the morning.

Dreams and the Body

NREM sleep (stages 1–4 in the chart) largely fitted the previous understanding of sleep as a restorative time in which your muscles relax and your breathing and heartbeat slow down. REM sleep is very different. Your brain is as active as when you're awake and your heart rate and breathing increase to reflect the vivid experiences you are having (hence the alternative name for REM, paradoxical sleep).

When you dream your body responds to the dream as if it were really happening. If you dream of

Dement discovered REM sleep occurs in 90-minute cycles and that everyone has four to seven such REM periods a night.

You are almost always "turned on" while dreaming. Men and women experience sexual arousal in 95 percent of REM sleep.

running, your brain commands your legs to move. If you dream of swimming, it commands your arms to do the proper stroke. So why don't you get up and run or swim? Because part of your spinal cord inhibits movement during REM sleep.

In some people, often middle-aged men who go on to develop Parkinson's disease, this part of the spinal cord stops working effectively. As a result, you can witness the strange spectacle of people acting out their dreams. One man dreamed of being at a swimming pool and dived off his bed. (This kind of movement in sleep needs to be distinguished from sleepwalking and sleep talking, which happen during NREM sleep. If you wake someone up while he is sleepwalking, he'll have no idea of what he is doing. This is very different from waking someone during REM sleep. She'll know exactly what she is doing – chasing a robber, fleeing an earthquake, etc.)

One final fact that not many people know: you are almost always "turned on" while dreaming. Men and women experience sexual arousal in 95 percent of REM sleep. This is completely irrespective of whether there is any sexual content to your dreams. I've always understood this fact to confirm that dreams reflect your deepest desires.

Dream Recall

Dement discovered that every REM period was followed by a gross bodily movement (GBM) – meaning that a person would shift his arms, legs or position. When Dement woke people during the

REM period, they would remember a dream. If he woke them just after a GBM, most of the dream had gone. A minute or two later, and very little of the dream was left.

This has important implications for dream recall, as I indicated in chapter 1. If you want to remember a dream, you need to wake up *during the dream*. For maximum recall, you must stay still, gather the dream together, and then record it as quickly as possible without any intervening movement. Dream recall is very state-specific – even the most vivid dreams fade quickly if not recorded.

Dream Deprivation

Early experimenters attempted to find the purpose of REM sleep by depriving people of it – by waking them at the start of each REM cycle. Such "dream deprivation" experiments were widely reported, as were their results – that without REM sleep, subjects became increasingly disturbed and psychotic. Subsequent research has failed to confirm these earlier findings. Though we all have experience of being sleep deprived and how it affects our judgment, reactions and sense of well-being, it is not true that without dreams we become psychotic.

REM in the Womb

From about 30 weeks' gestation, the fetal brain is activated as in REM sleep. In fact, a fetus spends almost 24 hours a day in this state during the latter part of gestation. Is he dreaming? No one knows, although we can imagine there is a great deal of kinesthetic and auditory information to be processed as he moves about inside the womb and responds to the motion of his mother, and listens to his mother's heartbeat and the muffled sounds of the outside world.

At birth, a baby is in a REM state for about 16 hours a day. Most of the time a baby spends asleep, he spends in REM. From this peak, the amount of time we spend in REM sleep gradually declines as we get older. It is hard to escape the conclusion that REM helps the brain develop. In particular, there is evidence that REM is involved in helping us file and order our memories and learning.

REM in Animals

All mammals (even the most primitive and ancient ones, such as opossums) have sleep patterns that include REM sleep. If they have eyes, they have REM. This seems to indicate an evolutionary purpose to REM. Mammals, being warm blooded, needed to develop a means of keeping their temperature steady. Normally, our temperature is maintained within a degree of 37°C. Our brains are critically affected by temperature variations. If we get too cold, we lose coordination, and if we are too hot, our brains slow down. Hence the need for a siesta in hot countries – to reduce activity and thus body temperature.

Insofar as we can tell, REM is linked to the ability of mammals to maintain their temperature within certain limits. REM sleep is the one time during the day or night that mammals' bodies don't maintain a constant temperature. It is as if this "off period" is necessary to reset and sustain our temperature control mechanisms.

If rats are deprived of sleep for two weeks, they lose the capacity to control their own temperature, and their immune systems break down. They die from simple infections.

NREM Dreams

In the original research on REM, it was discovered that when you wake up people during NREM sleep, they

All mammals (even the most primitive and ancient ones, such as opossums) have sleep patterns that include REM sleep.

would recall dreams roughly 10 percent of the time. For some time it was assumed that these were dreams from REM sleep, and somehow remembered later. By the 1960s, it became increasingly clear that this assumption was wrong, and that some dreams happened during NREM sleep, especially immediately after you fall asleep and in the early morning just before you wake up. These dreams could not be distinguished from REM dreams.

In 1997, the psychoanalyst and neuro-psychologist Mark Solms published research that changed the debate on dreams and REM. Working at Bart's Hospital in London, Solms studied patients whose brains had been damaged, often by strokes. He was particularly interested in the effect of highly localized brain damage on the patient's dreaming.

His first finding was that damage to the pons, the part of the brain that produces REM sleep, did *not* affect people's ability to dream. Patients who had no REM sleep frequently reported dreams.

He discovered that what did affect a person's ability to dream was damage to the area of the forebrain associated with desire and motivation (the ventromesial quadrant). Patients who have had this bit of the brain damaged are unable to initiate action. They more or less sit in a chair until they are told to do something.

In other words, if there is no desire, there are no dreams. This finding is uncannily reflected in our language. We often use the word "dream" in place of desire – our "dream house", "dream job", "dream car". It is as if our language foreshadowed this

DREAM PARALYSIS

We all have had the experience of being frightened in a dream and wanting to scream, run, kick or punch – and of being unable to do so because we are unable to move in the dream. J. Alan Hobson, a dream researcher, believes this experience is due to the fact that while dreaming we are literally unable to move because our bodies produce neural inhibitors, which stop us from acting out dreams. (Hobson also believes that the feeling of moving through molasses in dreams is due to the same cause.) Superficially, it seems like there might be some mileage to this explanation, but if it were true, why don't we feel paralyzed all the time in our dreams?

Some of us have had the experience of being paralyzed for what can seem a long time when we wake up – we literally find ourselves unable to move. This can be a very frightening experience. It's probably due to the fact that our spinal cord is still stopping us moving. If this happens to you, the way to bypass this inhibition is to think of moving your fingers or face muscles – the inhibition is much more profound with large muscle groups, as it's aimed at keeping you from getting out of bed and moving around.

important discovery. Equally, Solms' research confirms my experience of working with dreams – dreams are enormously responsive to your desires. If you want a dream about a particular problem or issue, a psychic dream or a lucid dream – ask and your dreams will respond.

Solms found the other area of the brain that affected people's capacity to dream was the part of the forebrain that is associated with spatial awareness and imagery. If this area (the parieto-temporo-occipital [PTO] junction) is damaged, again, you don't dream.

We now know both from Solms' research and new studies using PET and MRI scans that while the

In other words, if there is no desire, there are no dreams.

brain is as busy dreaming as awake, different parts of the brain are active in both states.

Chemicals and Dreaming

We have already discovered that the parts of the brain that are active during REM sleep are different from those that are active when we're awake. Equally important, however, is the chemical environment in the brain, which affects how the neurons fire.

While we are awake, the chemicals that predominate in our brain are noradrenalin and serotonin. They are associated with reflective thought, straight-line thinking, and the ability to concentrate. Most of us will know these chemicals for their effect on mood, through such drugs as Prozac, which are selective serotonin reuptake inhibitors (SSRIs). Such drugs increase the amount of serotonin in the gaps between nerve cells.

In NREM sleep, the amounts of serotonin and noradrenalin in the brain are reduced by half. In REM sleep, by 100 percent. In their place, a different set of chemicals flood the brain, especially those areas that are active during dreaming. These "cholinergic" chemicals provide a totally different environment for the neurons in the brain, accentuating strong emotions and the ability to make connections between thoughts.

Creativity and Dreaming

In other words, during REM sleep (where most dreams happen), the chemicals that are associated with logic and reflective thought are reduced to nothing, and chemicals that help make unusual associations or connections are greatly increased. Being creative involves making unusual connections between thoughts or facts. Being creative also often

SENSORY INFLUENCES ON DREAMS

Most of us have had the experience of an alarm being incorporated into our dreams. This makes it logical to assume that dreams could be affected by external influences. Before the discovery of REM, early dream researchers such as Maury tried to discover whether you could affect dreams in this way. Maury found that when he had a hot iron brought near his face, he dreamed that people were trying to extract money from him by putting his feet near hot coals. In another experiment, he had water dripped on his forehead and dreamed of sweating profusely.

After the discovery of REM, similar experiments were tried during REM periods. Buzzers were sounded, smells were introduced, dreamers were touched with various objects. Contrary to popular belief and the early informal experiments, it proved enormously difficult to affect people's dreams. (With an EEG, you can see the brain registering the disturbance, much as it does when awake. But the noise, smell, or touch doesn't make it into the dream.)

involves setting aside ideas about how things should be done and what is supposed to happen (thinking "outside the box"). In REM sleep, our ability to do both is greatly enhanced. *This is why dreaming is potentially the time of our peak creativity.*

Dreams and Memory

We also have evidence that the brain uses the hyper-associative state of REM sleep to accomplish an important task involving our memory.

Every day we are exposed to huge amounts of information. Some of it we are aware of taking in – for example, the quickest route to the bus stop or that our partner prefers whisky to sherry. This is called declarative memory – facts we can say (declare). But a great deal of what we take in every day we could not describe or declare. This could involve skills or procedures that are very difficult to describe (how to ride a bike), or knowledge we take in subliminally – e.g., the non-verbal cues that help us tell someone's smile is false.

We can hold an enormous amount of material in our short-term memories, which lasts up to a week. But we cannot hold everything we learn and remember in our consciousness – there is simply too much material. So we need a process through which short-term memory is transformed into long-term memory, a process through which short-term memory is linked to other bits of information, other skills, other procedures we have already stored long term. This seems to occur at least partially during the dream state.

The way our memory works is through association. You've probably experienced an example of this when you try to remember the name of an actor or actress. "It begins with a B," you'll say. "And he was in that movie about … drugs, the one where that Welsh girl played the wife … It had a short title, *Traffic*, that's it. *Traffic*. It's like a bull – his name's got something to do with bulls … Del Toro, yeah, Benicio Del Toro."

First you tried sound and spelling, but that drew a blank, then you tried a movie he was in, still a blank, then an associative meaning – bulls, el toro, Del Toro, you got there.

We've already established our brains are flooded with chemicals that promote associativity during REM sleep. This unique state allows associations to be made between our new short-term memories and our longer-standing memories. Once this link is made, their presence in our short-term recall is no longer required, and we can access them by a process something like the one described above.

There is much experimental evidence that a night's sleep is what allows our memories to be consolidated into our long-term recall.

TO SUM UP

Scientific research can't tell us everything about dreams, but it has established important facts that need to be part of any theoretical understanding. Some of the crucial ones are:

- Dreaming is as real to the body as waking. Our eyes follow the action and our legs and arms register movement. When we "run", our heart rate goes up and our breathing becomes more rapid.
- Dreams are indelibly associated with desire. If the part of the brain associated with desire is damaged, we don't dream. Further evidence of this is the way we are "turned on" physically by most dreams, whether sexual in content or not.
- While our brains are as active while dreaming as when awake, different parts are active. This is largely because of the different chemical environment in those parts of the brain. Chemicals associated with reflective thought and straight-line thinking are reduced to zero. Chemicals associated with emotion and the ability to make connections are greatly increased. Since creativity comes from making unusual connections, dreaming is a time of peak creativity.
- The brain also uses this different chemical environment to perform another function. It seems dreaming and REM sleep are the times when we consolidate short-term memory into long-term memory. We do this by using our hyper-associative state of mind to connect new meanings to older ones already in our long-term storage. In other words, we make those associative links that help us to access and retrieve information.
- Dream images are made by a brain in maximum associative mode. It seems likely that the ability to associate will be important in making sense of dream images.

3

Dream Creativity

Solution Dreams

I was 20 years old, in my fourth year at university, when I had my first indication of how dreams can help when you're stuck for an answer to a problem.

I'd won a playwriting competition in my third year. Emboldened by this, I told my friends I'd win the major competition – open to graduate students – the next year. It was two weeks before the competition deadline and I had a small problem. I had no idea what I was going to write.

To forget my troubles, I went to a party. While talking to a total stranger, in the middle of a conversation about something completely different, she suddenly said, "Isn't 'Cantata for Two Kazoos and a Jew's Harp' a great title for a short story?" Rather stunned, I agreed it was a great title and

asked if I could borrow it. No problem. I went to bed that night thinking, "I've got a terrific title. Now all I need is a story!" In the morning, I woke up with a vivid dream giving me the plot to a story that fit the title perfectly. I wrote the play and won a major Hopwood Award.

This experience aroused my curiosity. I started reading and discovered that I was far from the first person to have such a problem-solving dream. In fact, versions of what had been called dream incubation were common in the ancient world (see box, below). Many modern dreamers too had had

DREAM INCUBATION

Imagine a world in which everyone believed that dreams were given by the gods. And that the gods could appear in the dreams of ordinary people.

This was the world of the Ancient Greeks. And it led to a dream practice that produced healings so miraculous they are hard for us, the inheritors of the Greek intellectual tradition, to credit today.

To understand this practice, let's look at Epidaurus, one of the sanctuaries of Aesclepius, the healing god of the Greeks. It was active from the 6th century B.C. to the 3rd century A.D. – 900 years.

The sanctuary at Epidaurus consisted of a large, beautiful sacred precinct, composing not just a temple but a magnificent theatre, places for the supplicants to stay, bathe and eat. People came to the temple with a wide variety of mental and physical ailments – from insomnia to blindness to infertility.

If you were ill, you would undertake the long journey to the sacred precinct. There, a priest would admit you after a ritual cleansing bath. You would then participate in the life of the sanctuary – attending theatre, poetry readings and even sporting contests if you were able –

until you were judged ready to enter the temple and sleep in the *abaton*, the special chamber within, for one night only.

Abaton literally means "place not to be entered unbidden". How was it decided you were bidden? You'd keep careful records of your dreams until there was a coincidence between one of your dreams and the dream of a priest. This was the sign you were ready. You'd make a sacrifice to the god and be led into the temple where you'd sleep on a pallet.

In the early years of the temple it was expected that you'd have a dream that would heal you on the such dreams, in which solutions to problems that had bedevilled them appeared as if by magic. My work, and that of others, has shown that you can teach people to have Solution Dreams, that the ability to dream up an answer to your problem is something everyone can develop.

I will explain how you do this in the next section. Here, I'll talk about the advantages of approaching dreams in this way and give a number of examples of Solution Dreams.

Creative Dreams

The melody of Paul McCartney's song *Yesterday* came to him in a dream. He was 22 and in London filming *Help!* One morning he woke up with a haunting tune in his head. He picked out the melody on a piano near his bed, all the while thinking it couldn't be his because he'd never written anything like it.

He tried playing the music to friends. No one recognized it. After a while, he realized it was really "his". He called it *Scrambled Eggs*. His provisional lyric went, "Scrambled eggs, oh, my baby, how I love your legs…"

McCartney wrote the lyrics we know some time later. "It's the most complete thing I've ever written…" he said. "For something that just happened in a dream, even I have to acknowledge it was a phenomenal stroke of luck."

There's no question that *Yesterday* is far and away Paul McCartney's most popular song. It has been recorded by more than 3,000 artists and played on the radio many thousands of times more than any other recorded song. A real testimony to dream creativity!

A dream also inspired *Frankenstein*, perhaps the most famous horror story of all time. Mary Shelley (Wollstonecraft at the time) and her gang, which included Percy Shelley, Lord Byron and a number of others, had spent the evening telling ghost stories.

spot. Such healings happened every day for hundreds of years. In later years, you were occasionally given a sort of prescription in the dream – instructions to eat certain foods, take certain baths or prepare herbs to drink. No dream interpreters worked in the precinct, nor did the priests interpret dreams. *It was the dream itself, and the god's presence in it, which healed.*

After your dream, you'd erect a tablet telling your name, your disease and how you were cured. Hundreds of these tablets remain. Here are just two examples.

Euphanes of Epidaurus

This young boy had a stone in his bladder. While sleeping in the sanctuary, he had a dream that the god came to him and asked, "What will you give me if I cure you?" Euphanes replied, "Ten dice." The god laughed at the boy's cheek and told him he would heal him. In the morning, the boy was perfectly well.

Gorgias of Heracleia

This soldier had an arrow lodged in his lungs. His lungs became so inflamed that he filled 70 basins with pus. During his night in the sanctuary, he had a vision of the god coming and taking the arrow point from his lung. He walked out of the temple cured, holding the point in his hand.

Before they went to bed, Byron challenged them each to create a horror story of their own. Mary Shelley dreamt:

I saw the pale student of unhallowed arts kneeling beside the thing he had put together – I saw the hideous phantasm of a man stretched out, and then on the working of some powerful engine, show signs of life, and stir with an uneasy, half vital motion … [The Creator] sleeps but he is awakened; he opens his eyes, behold, the horrid thing stands at his bedside, opening his curtain and looking on him with yellow, watery, but speculative eyes …

Swift as light and cheering was the idea that broke in upon me, "I have found it! What terrified me will terrify others…"

And as we all know, this was indeed the case. Both the book and the subsequent adaptations for television and film have thrilled and scared people since *Frankenstein* was published in 1818.

Other famous examples of Solution Dreams are: Kekule, who discovered the structure of the benzene molecule, Elias Howe who invented the sewing machine and Otto Loewi whose dream won him a Nobel prize by enabling him to prove his theory of the chemical transmission of nerve impulses.

The problem with all these examples is that it's easy to think, "This is the kind of thing that happens to people like Paul McCartney and Mary Shelley, but not to someone like me." For this reason, most of the remaining examples in this chapter are not the classic examples usually given of Solution Dreams. Rather, I've chosen the dreams of people who learned the skill of having such dreams from workshops or classes.

Technical Solutions

The following dreams come from Deirdre Barrett's inspiring compilation of creativity in dreams, *The Committee of Sleep*. Both occurred to individuals who had learned the art of having Solution Dreams in creativity workshops at work.

Floyd Ragsdale, an engineer at Dupont, was inspired by such a course to start recording his own dreams.

Some time later, Dupont was given a large contract to produce Kevlar for the bullet-proof vests worn by American soldiers in the first Gulf War. They were managing to keep to a tight schedule until a machine broke down. No one knew what was wrong. The delay in production was costing Dupont $700 a minute and endangering soldiers' lives. Ragsdale was one of the many engineers assigned to fix it. At the end of a long day, he and the large team were no wiser as to what was wrong with the machine.

Going home exhausted, Ragsdale decided that this was his chance to have a Solution Dream. He asked for a dream telling him what was wrong with the machine and how to fix it. He fell asleep and dreamt he *was* the broken machine. Water was spraying everywhere and he saw springs and hoses. Water ran down the outside of the machine. When he awoke he wrote down two words, "hoses, springs".

In the morning, he contemplated these two words. Suddenly he had it! The problem with the machine was that the hoses feeding chemicals and water into it had collapsed internally. Coiled springs inside the hoses would be a cheap and effective way to fix them.

Ragsdale took his solution to his supervisor (omitting the fact that it had come to him in a dream). His supervisor was dubious that the hoses could be the problem. It wasn't until much later in the day, when everything else had failed, that he thought to try Ragsdale's idea. The engineers pulled out the hoses, and lo and behold, they had collapsed inside. Ragsdale fitted springs into them and the machine was back on line by the end of the day. This one dream saved Dupont millions of dollars.

Anjali Hazarika, a psychologist at India's National Petroleum Management Programme, runs dream creativity workshops for all its employees. Her idea is that dreams will help people solve their relationship problems – both personal and job-related – freeing up more energy for work and enabling work groups to function better.

Some of her students do not limit their dream creativity to this. One chemist was trying to develop a way of refining crude oil using enzymes. He asked for a dream to help him. In the very vivid dream that followed, he was standing by the side of a road when an old lorry loaded with rotten cabbages passed by. He could smell the stench of the cabbages. When the chemist awoke, he couldn't see how this dream was an answer to his question. Neither could the other chemists on his team (all of whom had taken the workshop). They explored the symbolism of cabbages but drew a blank.

It was a week later, when sitting at his workbench, that the penny dropped. He realized that cabbages, when they rot, are attacked by bacteria that produce precisely the enzyme he was looking for. He went on to develop a method of refining crude oil using this enzyme. And of course, rotten cabbages are a very useful raw material – they're cheap and easily available.

A friend of mine, Stephen, regularly has Solution Dreams but they're rather different from any I've encountered. In his dreams, he tries one approach after another in an experimental fashion, until he has one that works. He then decides to remember this in the morning. When I met him, he complained that because of his age he no longer could count on his memory – on several occasions he had woken up with only two of the three factors involved in a solution – so he now had to wake up and write it down.

On one occasion, Stephen and his family had moved into a new house. There was a medium-sized space for the kitchen but no one could figure out

EINSTEIN'S DREAM

When Albert Einstein was a teenager and failing at maths in school, his parents decided they should take matters in hand. They encouraged him to do a plumbing apprenticeship. It was during this difficult period of his life that Einstein had the dream that shaped his life's work.

"In his dream, he was sledding with his friends at night. They would climb the hill, whisk down the snowy slope, then climb to the top again… Einstein climbed the hill and started to slide down once again, only this time, he became aware that his sled was travelling faster and faster… he realized he and his sled were approaching the speed of light. He looked up at this point and saw the stars – they were being refracted into a spectra of colours that Einstein had never seen before. He felt filled with a sense of awe and numinosity [sic]. He understood that in some way he was looking at the most important meaning in his life." (From *Where People Fly and Water Runs Uphill*).

As he reflected on his life, Einstein said, "You could say, and I would say, that my entire scientific career has been a meditation on that dream!"

I find this dream fascinating for a number of reasons. Though clearly a kind of Solution Dream – it helped Einstein resist the pressure of his parents to become a plumber – it also expresses something that neither Einstein nor anyone else on the earth knew or understood. It's definitely not a Solution Dream that draws on existing knowledge or perceptions.

One of the major reasons we find dreams so difficult to understand is that we don't usually know the context in which they occur. It's like hearing an answer to a question but not knowing what the question is.

how they could get the four items they needed – a sink, a hob, an oven and a refrigerator – into the three spaces for them. A trail of carpenters and kitchen fitters admitted defeat. Stephen decided to take matters into his own hands. "It was a spatial problem," he said. "The kind I like playing around with in my dreams."

In his dream he tried one arrangement of the kitchen after another. Then he had his eureka moment – the fridge would fit in the chimney breast! He played around with the other shapes, fitted them in and decided to remember his answer in the morning. He did. It worked.

Personal Solutions

Though Jessica was crazy about her new boyfriend, she often found him distant and unavailable. And he had to travel a lot on business. After taking my workshop she asked for a dream about the future of the relationship. All she remembered that night was a fragment – she and her boyfriend were on the *Titanic*, in separate rooms.

Talking to the group, Jessica said she'd recently seen the movie on television – clearly that was why it occurred in her dream. When people suggested the *Titanic* was chosen to symbolize the future of the relationship, she scoffed. It was only day residue. And to prove it, she said, she'd ask for another dream.

In her second dream, she was again on the *Titanic*. But this time she was able to go into her boyfriend's room. To her surprise she found a family in it – and two small boys who bore a distinct resemblance to him. The next morning she asked her boyfriend whether he had a family. He

demanded to know who had ratted on him, and Jessica realized her dream was true.

The moral? If you are tempted to write off a Solution Dream as something that was triggered by an event during the day, think again.

James, who took another Solution Dreams workshop, was an architect unhappy in his job. He asked whether he should "take the plunge and throw in my current work which, though highly paid, gives me no satisfaction?"

He had two dreams the following night. In the first, he was looking through a long series of second homes in France on the internet. In the second:

I am high up on a horse-drawn or steam-driven wagon or float during a day-time street celebration – like an opening scene from a Wild West movie – town streets absolutely crowded with revellers on foot and vehicles winding around each other but moving slowly – streamers in the air and the sound of steam pipes and barrel organs. Carnival atmosphere. Strange detached dreamlike quality – all is viewed from above like an overhead camera shot. Don't feel directly involved (not revealing myself, more like an observer) as though I'm thinking "What's going on here?"

When James awoke he wrote off the first dream as a repetition of what he had been doing the night before (like Jessica) and he couldn't make any sense of the second.

When he told the dreams in the workshop, he realized that the scene reminded him of the forced frivolity and emphasis on "having a good time" in his workplace, and that his attitude in the dream was precisely what he felt at work, which was why he wanted to leave.

Interestingly enough, when James was made voluntarily redundant a short time later, he received a much bigger package than he'd expected. And this money was just enough to purchase a second home in a mountain village in Italy. Something at the time of the first dream he hadn't really contemplated.

Access to What You Know

In most of these Solution Dreams, the dream does two things:

1   It draws on the sum total of our perceptions, knowledge and experience to produce an answer to our question.
2   It uses a kind of associative thinking not limited by our usual notions of what works.

In my first Solution Dream, for example, the story that my dream produced was composed of various bits of my own life, suitably moulded to fit the title "Cantata for Two Kazoos and a Jew's Harp". Ragsdale, in his dream, drew on his intimate knowledge of the machine he was trying to repair and his subliminal perceptions – thinking so far outside the box that his supervisor initially rejected his solution.

As we showed in the previous chapter, the fact that our brains are in a hyper-associative state when we dream enables us to make huge numbers of connections – and thus draw on our accumulated conscious and unconscious knowledge. The fact that the chemicals usually associated with logical thinking are reduced to zero enables us to think more creatively and in less predictable ways.

But not all Solution Dreams fit into this model. In some dreams we access information no one knows, such as in Einstein's dream on page 35.

Every Night

Rosalind Cartwright, a psychologist and dream researcher studied the dreams of people who were depressed and/or in a crisis – recovering from a divorce or bereavement. She took people into a dream lab and woke them up after each dream. Over time, she observed a pattern. The first dream of the night seemed to state the problem. Each successive dream was a more complicated and imaginative attempt to solve it. The last dream of the night presented the most complete and fantastic solution.

Cartwright's work implies that we are always trying to solve problems in our dreams, but because we don't remember them or know their context, all this dream work goes to waste. Interestingly enough, she found that people who were severely depressed did not show this pattern of dream development – rather their later dreams were like their first, a restatement of the problem along with the feeling that it was impossible to solve. (We talk about the technique she developed to help in such cases in the box on page 104.)

Context

I suspect that one of the major reasons we find dreams so difficult to understand is that we don't usually know the context in which they occur. It's like hearing an answer to a question but not knowing what the question is.

When you ask your dream a question before you go to bed, this difficulty disappears – you know the particular context for your dreams of that night. This is one reason that Solution Dreams tend to be much easier to understand.

The ability to have a dream answer a day-world question also implies we can develop a dialogue with our dreams, based on the model of ordinary conversation. If you ask someone a question and they give you an answer you don't understand, you say, "Could you explain that?" or "Could you say that again, differently?" You can do the same things with dreams. If you have a Solution Dream (or any dream) that doesn't make sense to you, review the dream the following night and ask for a clearer response. Or if the answer leads you to another question you can ask that too. Soon you'll have a proper conversation going. It can be like having an immensely wise friend who's always on call.

How to Have a Solution Dream

About 20 years ago, I started to do workshops in which I tried to recreate the Greek practice of dream incubation in a modern setting, using guided fantasy, artwork and group exercises. These worked and the people in my workshops had some very powerful dreams, but after a while I began to wonder why I was going to so much trouble to recreate an experience which came easily to me. My experience, combined with my study of the incubation practices of the Greeks and other psychologists, led to the method described below.

There are several things that we can learn from the Greeks:

- Remembering and recording dreams. Doing this regularly was a prerequisite for sleeping in the *abaton* (see pages 32–3). The last thing you wanted was to waste the one and only night you were able to sleep there by not remembering a dream. Though you won't have only one chance to set up a Solution Dream, it's discouraging to spend the time and energy doing this and then not have a dream. To avoid this, get into the habit of remembering at least three or four dreams a week *before* doing the Solution Dream exercise.

- Readiness. The Greeks had the notion of being "ripe" for a healing dream. We clearly can't emulate their custom of comparing dreams with the temple priests to assess this, but we can develop more personal and subjective ways of determining our readiness to solve a particular problem (see Step 1 – Choosing an Issue).

- Belief. For the Greeks, the existence of the gods and their capacity to appear in dreams was a basic fact of life, confirmed by artifacts (clay tablets all around the temple), and their experience (that they, or someone they knew, had had a close encounter with a god). We cannot easily obtain this level of belief but the more we

work with dreams and experience their wisdom and creativity, the more powerfully our dreams can work.

- Testifying. It was part of the temple ritual to testify publicly about your healing dream. Speaking to sympathetic others about your incubation successes makes them more real and, over time, changes the climate of opinion about dreams.

Four Steps to a Solution Dream

Setting up a Solution Dream takes between 15 and 30 minutes. Don't skimp on this the first couple of times you set up a dream. You want to get a series of successful results under your belt before you start cutting corners.

Do this on a night when you don't have to get up early in the morning and when you haven't eaten or drunk too much in the evening.

Step 1 – Choosing an Issue

There are three basic rules for choosing what to have your first Solution Dreams about. Choose:

- An issue or problem that *engages your heart and mind*. Remember that without desire you don't dream. Engage your desire by asking something that matters to you. Something that will make a difference to you (and perhaps other people) and that will show you the power of your dreams.

- An issue you feel *ready* to have a solution to. Don't ask if you should change jobs, leave your partner or move to another city if you can't bear to get an answer other than the one you want. A rough way to assess this is to think what if I really had a solution to this problem – would I implement it? If not, ask another question.
- A question that you feel it is *possible* to solve. Don't use your first question to ask how to establish world peace, end climate change or change your boss's essential nature. Ask yourself – do I believe there is a solution to this problem? Again, if the answer is no, ask another question.

Step 2 – Immerse Yourself in the Problem

Once you have decided the problem, issue or question you want your dream to address, you need to spend at least 10 minutes considering the problem consciously. Do this in your dream diary or on a separate piece of paper. You have two broad aims. The first is to get a sense of how the problem or issue affects your life and those you care about – this reminds you of your emotional involvement in the issue. The second aim is to examine the problem fully, so that you feel you have done everything you can to solve it consciously. Having done this and having not come up with a solution, you are then ready to release it to your dream to solve. Our guiding image here is Dimitri Mendeleyev, who struggled into the night with the problem of how to order the chemical elements according to their atomic weights. Exhausted, he fell asleep at his desk and dreamt up the Periodic Table.

The best way to do this is to go over the history of the problem/issue, your attempts to solve it, how it affects you and others and how your world would be different if it were sorted. Use the following points as a guide:

- Define as best you can the problem/issue.
- When did it start? What is its history? How has it developed?
- What do you take to be the "causes"?
- Why is this issue important to you?
- How does it affect you or others? In particular, what are the negative effects? What are you (and others) deprived of by it?
- What solutions have you tried? Why haven't they worked? What other solutions occur to you? Why aren't they right?
- What are the obstacles to a successful solution? (Include yourself – your attitudes, habits, etc.)
- Define as best you can what a successful solution would need to accomplish.
- How would solving this problem change your life and the lives of others?
- Add to these questions any that occur that are specific to the problem or issue.

DREAM BRAIN TEASERS

One of the easiest ways to start using your dreams to solve problems is to pose yourself a brain teaser before you go to sleep.

Why not try the following two teasers? Both have been successfully solved in dreams.

- The letters O,T,T,F,F form the beginning of an infinite sequence. Find a simple rule for determining the successive letters. What are the next two letters of the sequence?
- Which two words both start and end with the letters "he?"

The answers to these teasers will be obvious once you get them but if you'd like to cheat, the answers are given upside down on page 41.

Step 3 – Reduce the Problem/Issue to a Single Sentence

In this step you sum up the problem/issue you want to solve in a single sentence question. However, often this isn't as easy as it sounds. Why not? It's a bit like the story of the genie who grants you three wishes … The first wish is that you're as rich as

Croesus and the mischievous genie grants this, but you find that you are locked in a cave and can't spend it. The second wish is that you're rich and you're free to spend it – but now you're 90 years old and in a wheelchair … etc. Your mind and your dreams aren't as mischievous as the archetypal genie, but they will answer the question you ask, which may not be the one you want to have answered.

To prevent this confusion, keep the question clear and to the point. Be positive. And give the dream space in which to work. Ask "How can I have a better relationship with my daughter?" not "What is wrong with my daughter?" If you want to understand something, ask about that. "I'll remember a dream that will help me understand my relationship with my boss." If you need to make a choice, ask a question about that. "Should I take the new job or stick with my old one?" If you need help

GOOD DREAM – BAD PRACTICE

Thanks to the wife of William Rose, we now know that the classic British film *The Ladykillers* (recently remade with Tom Hanks) was inspired by a dream. Rose woke up in the middle of the night having dreamt the plot to the movie.

He knew immediately it was a great idea and woke up his wife Tania to tell her about it. Tania, too, was thrilled. But then (and this is the bad practice bit) William went straight back to sleep. Tania was left holding the baby (figuratively). She couldn't get up and write it down because that would have disturbed her three-year old daughter – easily awoken and an epic crier. So she sat in bed the rest of the night, repeating to herself the plot William had told her. In the morning, he had completely forgotten the dream. If she hadn't remembered it, *The Ladykillers* would never have come into being.

Moral: don't burden your wife or anybody else with needing to remember your Solution Dream. Write it down.

with an emotional problem, emphasize this. "I'll remember a dream that will help me achieve closure on the loss of my husband." When you are finished, write your single sentence question in bold letters in your dream diary.

Step 4 – Prepare for Sleep

After you have finished the above steps, prepare for bed. Try not to make phone calls or answer emails – this will dissipate the energy you have directed towards solving the problem. Make sure your dream diary and pen are by your side. Lay down and turn out the lights.

Go over the problem and your deliberations about it in your mind. Think of your single sentence question. Now imagine as vividly as you can waking up with a Solution Dream. How would you feel if

SETTING UP A SOLUTION DREAM

- Choose an issue or problem that you are ready to solve and which engages your heart and mind.
- Immerse yourself in the issue for at least 10 minutes. The aim here is to feel you've done everything you can to solve the problem consciously.
- Sum up the problem in a single sentence. Avoid ambiguity and make sure it is the question you want answered.
- Go to sleep repeating your single sentence question preceded by a phrase such as "I will remember a dream that will tell me…" Repeat this phrase again and again, like a mantra, as you drift off to sleep.
- When you wake up during the night write down anything – however irrelevant it seems – you remember. Go back to sleep, repeating your mantra again.

your problem. In many cases, the answer will be clear. As we've emphasized earlier, Solution Dreams tend to be easier to understand because you know the question they are a response to.

If you still don't see how the dream is an answer to your question, tell a sympathetic friend the question and the dream answer. Do they see the connection?

Don't force it. If after working with the dream and telling a friend you still don't see how it's an answer to your question, ask again. As you lie in bed, go over in your mind the dream you've had and the question you've asked. Ask for another dream to clarify the answer.

You Can't See It

If you feel the dream does contain an answer but one that you can't see or understand, you will need to learn more about working with dreams. Start with either the following chapter, What We Can Learn from the Dream Theorists, or the two chapters on Working with Dreams.

this happened? What would you say/do? Who would you tell? Include all this in the image. Make the image as real as you can.

The final step is to make your chosen question into a mantra, which you repeat again and again as you drift off to sleep. "I will remember a dream that will tell me …" Fill in your question.

When you wake in the night, stay still. Reel in your dream. Write it down, or whatever fragments or images you remember in as much detail as you can. Don't worry at this point if it is a solution to your question. Just get it down.

Then go back to sleep with the mantra again in your mind, "I will remember a dream that will tell me …"

Write down as many dreams as you remember. In the morning, look at your dream(s) as the answer to

ANSWERS TO DREAM BRAIN TEASERS

- One dreamer dreamt of the face of a clock and when she woke up realized the answer was the numbers on its face: One, Two, Three, Four, Five are obviously followed by Six and Seven.
- I presented this at a business conference. One mother had a dream of her kids driving her crazy by turning up the television sound to the maximum. It gave her a headache. In another dream the same night, she dreamt of a friend who refused to get out of a car where she was grieving. She realized she was suffering heartache.

4

What We Can Learn From the Dream Theorists

The Major Dream Theorists

What is a dream? Why are they so hard to understand? What sense can I make of them? What methods will enable me to get at their meanings?

We all have answers to these questions in our heads – sometimes mutually contradictory answers. None of us come to dreams afresh. We've imbibed ideas from our parents, peers and the general culture. Some of us have struggled with our own dreams, and have hard-won insights from this struggle.

In this chapter, I aim to illuminate some of the answers to these "big" questions about dreams. They are important because our dream work and the insights we gain from it will follow from our understanding of what a dream is and what it can offer us.

An important part of what we get from working with dreams is an opportunity to reflect on the assumptions and perceptions that govern how we live our lives. I hope to encourage you to reflect on your understandings of dreams by exposing you to some of the most important dream theories of the twentieth century.

Theory. There's a word to chill the blood and blank the mind. It's usually translated as – boring, abstract, unintelligible. In fact, it comes from the Greek *theoria*, to consider, look at. Theory gives us different ways to see the world. When we look at the world differently, we see different things. In relation to dreams, different theories help us to see connections and meanings in dreams we have never seen before.

The power of our twentieth-century Western dream ancestors is that they changed the world of dreams for us. Few people took dreams seriously before Freud. Freud and Jung changed our understanding of ourselves and of dreams. In this they changed us and our dreams forever.

How did they accomplish this? They gave us a language with which to think and talk about dreams. Their texts helped us to see and understand dreams as manifestations of the unconscious. This gives dreams multiple layers of meanings. They also gave us a language to see dreams through – condensation, displacement, persona, shadow, etc. Both allowed us to see aspects of dreams that had previously been invisible to us. (Language doesn't just attach a label to something we already know. Learning a word often enables you to see something new. James Lovelock's use of the word "Gaia", for example, helped us see the entire earth in a new light, as a living, breathing, interconnected organism.) Freud and Jung's new

language showed us phenomena we could see and experience for ourselves.

One of the functions of language is to bring some aspect of the world into the light in this way. Every language brings different elements of the world to the fore and hides others. So when we look at dreams through Freud's language, we see the importance of sexuality and wishes in our dreams, but our need to grow spiritually is hidden. Jung brought out the latter, but obscured the poetry of dreams. Hillman brings out the poetry, and so on.

Each of these thinkers tries to get to grips with his predecessors. Each attempts to bring out a different view of what the others reveal, and conceal. This engagement is important to us because it helps us clarify our assumptions about dreams and how we see them.

Of course, these brief chapters are my engagement with my ancestors. Freud and Jung each have over 20 substantial volumes of writings. In this limited space, I can't hope to sum up their contribution. I've been selective, but have tried to be true to the spirit of each.

In particular, I have tried to illuminate their basic assumptions and the questions they tried to answer. Each theorist has a different stance, and that leads to their different insights. All have contributed greatly to my understanding of dreams, outlined in the next section of the book.

Let me say something about my choices. Freud and Jung will be familiar, if only in name, to all my readers. Hillman, Berry and Boss less so. I have chosen them because they try to stay with the life of the dream and challenge the hegemony of the "scientific" study of dreams, which spends most of its time speculating about supposed mechanisms in the mind that create dreams.

In the following pages, I try to show what each thinker helps us see in dreams, so that these insights can become part of our quest through the rest of the book. I've also included practical exercises, so that you can start to engage with their discoveries.

Freud – Analyzing Dreams

Sigmund Freud's *Interpretation of Dreams* was the father of all modern dream books. Before *IoD*, dream interpretation was associated with the popular dream "code" book. For example, if you dream of a snake, you will have bad luck. Because of this, intelligent people didn't take dreams seriously. Freud legitimized working with dreams. Many of his insights into dreams are as true and useful today as they were when *IoD* was written, over 100 years ago.

If you consider the context in which Freud was writing, in which writing seriously about dreams was the kiss of death to one's intellectual reputation, his first paragraph is breathtaking in its confidence:

In the pages that follow I shall bring forward proof that there is a psychological technique which makes it possible to interpret dreams, and that if this procedure is employed, every dream reveals itself as a psychical structure which has a meaning and can be inserted at an assignable point in the mental activities of waking life. I shall further endeavour to elucidate the processes to which the strangeness and obscurity of dreams are due and to deduce from those processes the nature of the psychical forces by whose concurrent or mutually opposing action dreams are generated.

Not only does Freud declare he will show every dream is meaningful, but also how the meaning was derived and why they are so hard to understand. Freud recognized that his book would help define the new age. Though the book was actually published in 1899, he insisted the publication date be 1900. Famously, it sold only 351 copies in its first six years, but its influence was enormous.

I'm not going to try to explain all of Freud here, or even everything in *IoD*. Much of Freud's interest in dreams was in trying to work out the mechanisms of dream creation and a universal basis for understanding the "unconscious mind". Here, I'm going to concentrate on what Freud said that is useful for those who are trying to understand their own dreams. In many ways, *IoD* is a ideal guide, as so many of the dreams Freud includes are his own, which he analyzed himself.

Free Association

What was the "psychological technique" Freud found that enabled him to make sense of dreams, both his own and his patients'? Freud called it *free association*. It's remarkably simple. First you break the dream up into its components. A component is a character, a place, a speech or an action in the dream. Then you say, or write, whatever comes into your mind in connection with this component. You go through the whole dream, bit by bit, using this procedure. This is an *analytic* approach – you break the dream into little pieces and then determine what each piece means.

For example, a place in the dream might remind you of your first kiss and then of the horrible way that relationship ended. A person might remind you of someone else with whom you'd had the most embarrassing moment of your life, Most often, though, there will be several thoughts, feelings or lines of thought associated with each element. You write them all down.

Of course, free association is not quite that easy. To really free associate you need peace and quiet, so that you can concentrate on what you're thinking and feeling. This means you have to allocate special time for it. More importantly you need to eliminate or suspend your inner censor – the part of you that examines your thoughts and says "that's stupid".

"that's irrelevant", "that's silly". You need to relax Reason's guard, as Freud puts it, and allow yourself to get into a creative state of mind. When you do this, you will find that thinking about the different components of your dream allows unexpected thoughts and feelings to emerge.

We'll do more exercises with free association later in the book, but why don't you try it with one of your recent dreams?

Dream Thoughts

When you've finished free associating to a dream, you'll have a list of components, and all the thoughts and feelings that have occurred to you in connection with each one. These associations are what Freud calls *dream thoughts*. He felt they were what was originally in your mind before the dream came into being – the raw ingredients of the dream, so to speak. Free association was a way of retracing your mind's steps back to this raw material from the dream itself.

The next stage in Freud's method was to look at the dream thoughts, or associations, and try to find common threads or elements. Is one topic, situation or character mentioned several times, in different associations? Does a common theme occur in several associations, or nearly all of them? This would be the basis for the interpretation of the dream.

For example, after seeing me for four months, a client dreamt that she had to wait a long time after

ringing the entry bell to my office. An old boyfriend let her in. When she got to my consulting room, I was being all smarmy and charming with a power-dressed supervisor, and ignoring her. Her association to the old boyfriend was that he was reliable for five months, then let her down. He was also all smarmy and charming with other people.

In this case, two sets of associations led to an old unreliable boyfriend. The dream expressed her fear that I had been reliable so far, but would soon disappoint her. That it was a boyfriend might well have referred to feelings occasioned by transference in therapy.

Specificity

Free association helps us understand the specificity of dreams. You do not just dream of a bench, or a house, or a room but a specific bench, house or room. The bench might remind us of the seat where we carved a heart with the initials of our first love, or the one where we ended a painful affair. Each of these associations makes it a very different bench. A room in a dream is not just a room but a specific room with distinct spaces, colours and furniture.

Not only does Freud declare he will show every dream is meaningful, but also how the meaning was derived and why they are so hard to understand.

It's almost as if the elements in our dream are there to refer us to something specific in our lives.

Each element can remind us of something different, and all these associations help us come to terms with the specific meaning the dream image has for us.

It's almost as if the elements in our dream are there to refer us to something specific in our lives – they are allusions, just like you might get allusions in poetry, novels or films. Freud's method reminds us that this allusion needs to be included in the interpretation of the dream. He would say it was why this specific location, action or character was included in the first place.

Day Residue

Often, while associating to a dream, you will arrive at a point of contact with your experiences from the previous day. This may be something significant (you lost your wallet) or may be something trivial (you had to wait five minutes in a doctor's waiting room). Freud believed that every dream contained an element from something that happened the previous day. He called this *day residue*.

Day residue was always something you hadn't slept on yet. However unimportant the residue felt during the day, the fact that you dreamed about it made it meaningful. For example, if your associations led to the way you waited for your doctor for five minutes, and another bit of the dream concerned your current partner, for whom you often wait considerably more than five minutes, the unimportant day residue was linked with your irritation about your partner.

While Freud felt day residue was literally to do with the previous day's events, I have found dreams often contain references to events several days earlier. This is why it's important when keeping your dream diary to make note of all the events that happened before you had your dream – so that you can make links to these.

Why Do We Have to Interpret Dreams?

Every dream theorist has to confront a basic issue – why is dream interpretation necessary? Why isn't the meaning of every dream completely obvious to us when we awaken? Why don't we just think, oh, that dream is telling me that I should watch my step with my boss? Or this dream is telling me that this man/woman is the one?

Freud's answer to this question is simple – we don't understand dreams because we are not meant to. While one part of your mind is trying to express itself, another part wishes to disguise this expression because it regards it as unacceptable, embarrassing or shameful. Freud makes a distinction between the dream as remembered – the *manifest* dream – and the *latent* dream-thoughts – its underlying meaning. For him, the manifest dream was the result of a concerted effort of disguise and distortion by the censor, a part of the mind that screens unacceptable thoughts from consciousness.

Whether you buy this understanding or not (and I am skeptical of it), Freud's description of the way

Freud believed that every dream contained an element from something that happened the previous day. He called this day residue.

COMPOSITE FIGURES

In dreams, we often have characters who remind us of two or more people at once. This may be because a dream figure has two distinct characteristics, both of which remind us of different people. Or we may simply wake up thinking someone could have been either our mother or our wife.

Freud believed composite figures can be interpreted in any of three ways; they could

- Represent an element common to both people. In a recent workshop, a woman dreamed of her PhD supervisor, but strangely he had very long legs. I asked "Who has long legs like that?" The woman immediately answered, "My previous supervisor had legs like that."
- Be indicating a displaced common element. For example, your dream brother-in-law makes a gesture exactly like your friend Jack. You can't see what they have in common. But you associate to both and remember a recent occasion when you'd spent an evening in the pub with Jack, who managed to avoid paying for a single drink. Earlier in the year, you'd been annoyed with your brother-in-law for the cheap presents he bought your kids for Christmas. The displaced common element here is meanness.
- Express a wished-for common element. For example, you might dream of your husband wearing a smart suit typical of your boss. If your boss is very dynamic, and your husband very wishy-washy, this composite figure could represent your wish that your husband be more like your boss.

the censor works is enormously helpful for people trying to understand their own dreams. For Freud, the censor works by condensation, displacement and the use of symbols.

Condensation

We see condensation when someone in a dream reminds us of several people at once; the man's beard makes you think of your brother, but his expression is just like that of the teacher you had at school. Or, when at one point in a dream, the house is your grandmother's, and at a later point, it's your's. These are what Freud calls "composite figures" (see box above) and their construction is the main way condensation works in dreams.

In condensation, several meanings are compressed into one image. Freud said you know this has happened because when you associate to an image, you usually have many lines of thought or feeling leading away from it. He thought that in dream formation these lines of thought are "condensed" by the unconscious mind.

The notion of condensation helps us understand why dreams can have many true meanings. (Freud calls this *overdetermination* – any dream image will have multiple meanings.) Dreams are enormously

SEXUAL SYMBOLS IN DREAMS

Freud is notorious for his long lists of sexual symbols, expressing the phallus (knives, guns), the vagina (boxes, rooms) and the act of intercourse (going up steep staircases, pumping up tyres). It's true this sort of instant interpretation doesn't do justice to the dream images. But what's more important is that it doesn't tell us anything new.

Freud wasn't an idiot. So what was he drawing our attention to here? Firstly, the enormous importance of sexuality in our lives. We're never too old to think about sex or to desire someone. Sex/the desire for love/the desire to possess someone and make them "ours" are all confused in our minds, and are among the driving forces of our existence.

Gender, too, is one of the most powerful forces in defining our world and our place in it. Men tend to be the heads of countries, companies and other institutions. It's this potential power and potency that Freud means by the phallus – a phallic symbol refers to one's drive, potency, power. Similarly, a vaginal symbol refers to potential creativity, fecundity and capacity to love. Sexual intercourse can be everything from heaven to hell, but however it is experienced, it is one of the peak experiences in our lives.

It is always important when you see an image as a phallic symbol to look at the specificity of the image. A rusty old rocket ship may indeed be a phallic symbol, but it's very different from a shiny new Ferrari …

economical – they express so much meaning in what would otherwise seem a simple image. Our respect for the aptness of dream images only increases the more we work with dreams. We begin to see there is always a reason for putting this familiar chair in an unfamiliar room – it's never random.

Displacement

The censor also works by displacing meaning. What seems important in the dream may not be so important in the dream interpretation. When an emotion is associated with one event in a dream, it may have been displaced from another event. What you spend most of the time dreaming about may be relatively insignificant and an isolated image may be the key to the meaning of the dream.

In other words, the idea of displacement is based on a suspicion about the dream as you remember it. Freud doesn't believe you can trust the emphasis of the manifest dream. This is one of the most profound differences between Freud and other dream theorists. I think that Freud's emphasis on displacement has a lot to do with the fact that he "cut his teeth" interpreting his own dreams.

When you work with your dreams, often things that would be obvious to other people are not obvious to you. For example, you tell a dream to some friends and they exclaim, "That guy's acting just like your brother!" As soon as they say it, you realize it's true and you wonder how you didn't see it yourself. While I don't believe an unconscious mind "displaces" meaning from one thing to another in creating the dream in order to disguise its meaning, it is often the case that when you look at your dreams, your attention is "displaced". You don't see what's obvious. So when working with your dreams it's often good to be a bit suspicious if the dream seems to be completely transparent and is telling you something you already know.

Symbols

Freud says that some elements of the dream do not lead to associations. The dream interpreter draws a blank on them. Often, these elements are symbols. You will see as we go through the different dream theorists that each has a different understanding of symbols. You can learn something from each understanding, as they will illuminate the meanings of some of your dreams.

Freud is (in)famous for his long lists of symbols that are to be interpreted as the male or female sex organs, or as men or women. For example, "all elongated objects, such as sticks, tree trunks and umbrellas (the opening of these last being comparable to an erection) may stand for the male organ – as well as all long, sharp weapons, such as knives, daggers and pikes ... Boxes, cases, chests, cupboards and ovens represent the uterus, and also hollow objects, ships and vessels of all kinds." Such lists have been used by opponents of Freud to say that he reduces everything to sex. Freud said clearly that all symbols were not necessarily to be interpreted in this way. (See box, opposite).

Wish Fulfillment

Freud believed that after you had associated to and analyzed a dream – had discovered the disguised meaning beneath the manifest dream – you would always find a wish that was not fulfilled. A wish could be something as simple as, I wish I'd not drunk that last bottle of wine; I wish I hadn't married so hastily; or, as in Freud's own analysis of his specimen dream, "I wish I hadn't been responsible for what happened to this patient". Wish-fulfillment has been much misunderstood, and because of this, easily dismissed. Freud does not do himself any favours by going to extraordinary lengths to prove every dream was ultimately a wish fulfillment.

For Freud, the wish that the dream conceals is only present in the latent dream thoughts, not the manifest content (except in the case of children's dreams, which are relatively undisguised). So it's no good saying "This was a nightmare, how does that fulfill a wish?" For him, the nightmare is only the manifest content (see box, below). But Freud went further than this. He felt every wish in the dream ultimately connected with an infantile desire, the desire for love, the desire for the breast, or the desire to possess the mother/father without competition. It was this unfulfilled infantile desire that gave the wish the "power" to drive the formation of a dream.

I don't think that every dream is primarily aimed at expressing a wish, but I do think the concept of wish fulfillment is very useful to us in interpreting dreams. What Freud was getting at is that dreams come from the deepest part of our being. (He would have been delighted by the scientific evidence that without desire we cannot dream.) Our desires and wishes are enormously important for us – they drive us to take part in the world, And yet, these desires and wishes are often felt to be "wrong", "shameful"

or "unacceptable" because of cultural conditioning and our early experiences. Our dreams are not concerned with what is acceptable, but only with what is true. So these unacceptable feelings – a wish for revenge, a wish to kill those who get in our way, lust for people we're not "supposed" to desire etc. – do come into our dreams in ways we often find difficult to recognize. This might not necessarily involve the mechanisms that Freud described, but he did pinpoint the phenomena and the importance of our desires in our dream and waking life.

TYPICAL DREAMS

Examination Dreams

How many times do we have to resit exams/tests/essays in our dreams? We don't know where they are, we've not done the course work, we haven't prepared for them at all. Whatever, we know we're bound to fail and we wake feeling anxious, frightened and dismayed.

Freud says the key to understanding these dreams is that we never dream of exams we've actually failed, only tests we've passed. We dream of them when we're facing a challenge in our lives that raises anxiety for us – will we be equal to it? Or we have such dreams when we've done something wrong or failed to do something properly, and expect to be punished for it.

What do these dreams signify? Basically, they aim to reassure us. By putting us in a position where we were anxious and yet came through with flying colours, they are saying "Don't worry. You will pass this test like you passed the previous one." These dreams are examples of how a nightmare can represent a wish fulfillment.

Carl Jung

Originally a disciple of Freud's, and at one point Freud's heir apparent, Jung broke away to found his own school, Analytical Psychology. His influence on dream work is enormous, and most popular books on dreams reflect it and his assumptions. His connection with the human growth movement has further increased his appeal. Here, as with Freud, I will only sample Jung's views, concentrating on those that have been most influential in dream work.

Jung's work with dreams contains two conclusions that were fundamentally different from Freud's. First, he decided dreams were not meant to be hard to understand. Second, he felt that in dreams the unconscious mind aims to regulate our conscious attitudes and perceptions. Both these assumptions make dreams much more accessible to the ordinary individual.

Dreams as Language

Jung agrees with Freud that dreams can be hard to understand. He disagrees as to why. Jung believes the unconscious doesn't attempt to hide the meaning of the dream. Rather, he uses the metaphor of a text in a different language. If you try to read a Hittite text you can't make sense of it but not because the Hittites attempted to conceal its meaning. It's simply because you don't know the language. To get a sense of someone's dream language, Jung insisted on working with a series of dreams.

The idea of dreams as a different language gives us a very useful metaphor for working with dreams – it's like learning a new language.

Present and Future

Freud's dream analysis invariably takes you into the past to where he feels the desire that underpins the dream originates. Jung takes a different stance. He understands dreams to be a product of the present, aimed at the future. Jung sees dreams as an ongoing commentary from the unconscious mind on our present circumstances and understanding. This commentary can have pointers towards the future, or at least indications of the consequences of continuing on our present path.

This understanding of dreams as basically corrective – in that they correct conscious understandings – has several major consequences. It implies that dreams are in a constant dialogue with your consciousness. You can learn from this dialogue by tuning into your dreams. Even people who are not "into" Jung are influenced by the idea that dreams are part of personal development. Books like this are one of the consequences.

Compensation

How do dreams work to correct conscious understandings? Jung's answer to this question is that dreams have a compensatory function. If you have a one-sided view of a situation or person, they show you the other side. Let's say you're proud of yourself for your moderation, but have a series of dreams in which you stuff yourself with food and drink copious amounts of alcohol.

The idea here is not that the dream is saying, "you are really a pig". Rather the dream aims at showing you are both moderate and immoderate. This *and* that, rather than this, *not* that. It is a question of assimilating the new idea, without destroying the old one, of being able to hold both ideas in the mind at once.

Compensation in dreams can operate in a variety of ways. One is by exaggeration. For example, if you think your lover is without faults, your dream may show them walking on water. Here the dream is saying, "Sure, your lover is so brilliant he/she walks

He understands dreams to be a product of the present, aimed at the future.

on water. Pull the other one." This exaggeration might be positive, as here, or negative, for example, if you dreamed of your partner as a homeless drunk.

Jung believes the amount of exaggeration present gives you a measure of how one-sided your conscious attitude is – the more exaggeration, the more one-sided the attitude to be balanced. This can be seen most clearly in series of dreams. The first dream in the series might show your perfect partner making a number of small mistakes, but if you don't get the message, the last dream portrays them as a complete buffoon.

Jung thus speaks of a teleological aspect of the

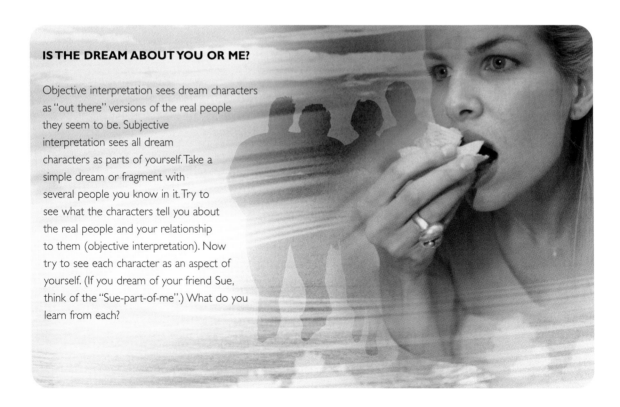

IS THE DREAM ABOUT YOU OR ME?

Objective interpretation sees dream characters as "out there" versions of the real people they seem to be. Subjective interpretation sees all dream characters as parts of yourself. Take a simple dream or fragment with several people you know in it. Try to see what the characters tell you about the real people and your relationship to them (objective interpretation). Now try to see each character as an aspect of yourself. (If you dream of your friend Sue, think of the "Sue-part-of-me".) What do you learn from each?

unconscious – it aims to correct, compensate and improve our conscious functioning. Dreams are not just regressive, a retreat into the past, or concerned with wish fulfillment. They are purposeful and have the goal of helping you.

Individuation

Compensation is part of a larger picture of how dreams can be part of our growth and development. For Jung, the aim of one's life is to strive for a wholeness, a becoming more oneself. Working with dreams is a major way to achieve this process of individuation. Through compensation, a balance between the opposites in our personality and perceptions can be achieved. Individuation is an inner drive to become a better rounded person.

Individuation involves a process of becoming conscious of, and integrating, unconscious aspects of oneself, and of developing those aspects of your personality that are undeveloped. "The individuated human being is just ordinary … He will have no reason to be exaggerated, hypocritical, neurotic … He will be in 'modest harmony with nature …'" This goal is very much like Freud's goal of psychoanalysis – "to turn neurotic misery into ordinary human unhappiness".

But unlike Freud's goal, individuation has a spiritual dimension. Jung was more comfortable with the idea of spiritual development than Freud (his father was a pastor) and he had many powerful religious experiences during his life. For Jung, individuation was a spiritual path, an understanding influenced by his study of Eastern religions.

Compensation in dreams can operate in a variety of ways. One is by exaggeration.

QUESTIONING JUNG'S CONCEPTION OF THE UNCONSCIOUS

Numerous writers have questioned the way Jung's predilection for inventing psychic entities (psyche, archetypes and so on) and the way he thinks about the unconscious. His theories end up positing an unconscious mind that has all the powers normally attributed to God:

- It can be aware of and judge what we're doing and how appropriate it is.
- It can figure out what we need to grow and develop, and
- It provides a path to realize this.

Having created such a powerful entity, Jung then creates a series of psychological structures and mechanisms to "explain" how it works.

The notion of compensation is a good example. Does the unconscious mind really compensate? Rather, many people would argue dreams show your situation at the moment. Any messages we draw from this – the idea that the lover who walks on water compensates for our conscious attitude – are an interpretation. Compensation doesn't happen *in* the dream. It happens when we reflect on the relation of the dream to our waking attitude.

If we see compensation as part of our consideration of the dream when we're awake, we're less likely to get involved in attributing God-like powers to the "unconscious mind".

The Collective Unconscious

Jung's idea of the collective unconscious is one of his major departures from Freud. From his experience of working with schizophrenics at the Burgholzli Mental Hospital, he became convinced that some elements of the dreams and visions of these very disturbed individuals bore an uncanny resemblance to obscure ancient religious rites and alchemical texts, to which they couldn't possibly have had access. Jung hypothesized that these schizophrenics

They are purposeful, and have the goal of helping you.

were tuning into archaic residues of human experience, and that these residues were part of our human inheritance.

This led him to the assumption that the unconscious mind had two components, the personal unconscious, largely explored by Freud, and the collective unconscious, containing the inherited experience of mankind.

The collective unconscious is composed of two elements, the instincts and the archetypes. Instincts have a biological quality and are often manifest not so much in a thought but in action – the flight or fight syndrome, or the love of a mother for her offspring. Instincts, if you like, are often bodily and can be experienced as overpowering – as in a gut instinct, for example.

Archetypes and the Structure of the Psyche

Archetypes are the carriers of the archaic residue of human experience. They can be best understood as psychic templates of understandings inherited from the experience of many previous generations of man. You can't experience an archetype directly. Rather, Jung assumes their existence to explain the occurrence of thoughts and images that he considers to be common throughout mankind.

Archetypes were important for Jung, because they helped delineate what he saw as the structure of the *psyche*. For Jung, the psyche is the totality of all psychological processes – both conscious and unconscious. He likened it to a boiling cauldron of contradictory impulses, inhibitions and emotions. Jung believed certain distinct conscious archetypal structures were in counter-point to equally distinctive unconscious archetypal components. The

conscious ego versus the unconscious shadow, the conscious public face (persona) versus the unconscious image of your soul (anima/animus) and so on (see box, opposite).

The archetypes are ordering principles that underpin the structure of the psyche. In dreams, Jung found archetypal images that would help him decipher what was going on in the psyche at any given time. For example, if the image of a cave or a rose recurs in a man's dreams, Jung might interpret them as being created by the mother archetype, or as an image of the anima. Whatever occurs in the dreams with the caves or roses would then be descriptive of what is happening with the man's psychic state.

You don't just know an archetypal image by the experience of it, but by research you (or others) have done into how similar images occur in different cultures, religions and rituals. For example, many myths and cultures have a character such as the Wise Old Man/Woman (Merlin) or the Eternal Youth (Peter Pan). He/she may assume slightly different forms in different cultures, but has many characteristics in common.

Subjectively, an archetypal image has an emotional grip on us – it is this emotional charge that is, for Jung, the indicator of an archetypal energy behind the image. It is both a sign of the presence of the archetype, and a manifestation of its power. In ancient times, this emotional grip was seen as a sign of the presence of the gods.

In practice, archetypal images often seem to have

For Jung, individuation was a spiritual path, an understanding influenced by his study of Eastern religions.

Understanding Your Dream

There can be many interpretations to a dream, and each can lead to a different understanding. Using some of Jung's concepts, take a recent dream and try to locate the following archetypes. Does doing this exercise change how you understand your dream? In what ways?

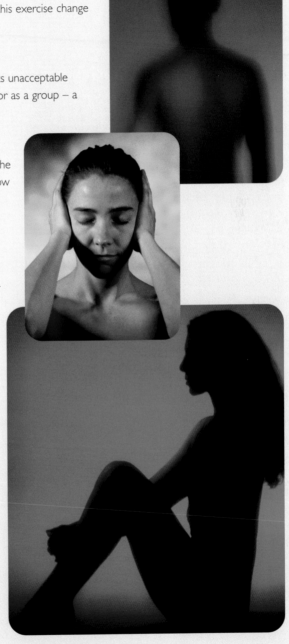

1 **The Shadow**
The Shadow is the same-sex figure who represents unacceptable aspects of yourself. It may appear as an individual or as a group – a violent gang, for example.

2 **The Persona**
Literally from the Latin for mask (*persona*), this is the mask we present to the world, our public face. How is this presented in the dream?

3 **The Anima/Animus – Images of the Soul**
If you're a man, and dream of a woman who is in some way fascinating, she might represent your anima. Its meaning is composed of three strands – your experience of women, your feminine side and the inherited collective image of woman. For Jung, the anima represents *Eros* (the sexual instinct).

If you're a woman and dream of a man to whom you are attracted, he could represent your animus. The animus represents *Logos* (reason), the search for knowledge and truth.

It might appear in a variety of forms:
• A group of men (a gathering of judges or wise men);
• An individual man – father, husband, teacher or judge;
• A voice that conveys a sage comment or a general wise observation.

the same function for Jung as sexual symbols did for Freud – they were a place where personal associations were felt to be inadequate, and the therapist could come in with his own theory. Jung's extensive research into astrology, alchemy and ancient religions and rites meant that he could amplify at great length any image he felt was archetypal.

SYMBOLS OF THE SELF

The Mandala

The mandala comes originally from Tibetan Buddhist tradition. Mandalas are meant to be meditated on, and are created for rituals of initiation. They often depict a palace with four gates, facing the four corners of the world. In the centre of the mandala is usually a picture of a Buddhist deity – a different deity for each initiation.

Jung found images, which he took to be like mandalas, in many religious and mystical traditions, his own dreams and visions, and those of his patients. This led him to conclude that mandalas were a universal symbol of an inner development of the psyche, an archetype of the Self.

People influenced by Jung find themselves dreaming of mandalas and find it useful to follow his path in drawing, painting, sculpting and meditating on these symbols, giving form to a spiritual path. I have always found mandala imagery rare in those not influenced by Jung.

Amplification

Let's say you told Jung of a dream in which there was a crocodile. He'd first encourage you to produce personal associations to this image – it might remind you of a recent visit to the zoo, or a book of pictures you showed your child, etc. You'd try to make sense of the image in the light of these subjective amplifications. After you'd done this, Jung would help you see the meaning of the crocodile in different cultures. Objective amplification is the process through which archetypal meanings would be brought to bear on a dream or dream symbol. For Jung, part of the value of seeking links with outside ritual and knowledge was that it helped individuals connect with a larger world (often spiritual or divine), an experience that could be healing.

The Self and Individuation

The Self is the most important archetype, and Jung speaks of it as the archetype that subsumes all others. A symbol of the Self is an image representing this archetype, for example, the mandala (see box).

Jung gives several accounts of long series of dream fragments and visions, which he expands in terms of his alchemical and other knowledge. These accounts demonstrate, he believes, the way that the symbols of the Self exist in an autonomous way. There is no attempt to show that the change in the symbols accords with any other progress we might recognize and expect – for example, becoming wiser, happier, more accepting of oneself and others. In these essays, Jung seems to argue for a kind of individuation that occurs simply through the development of symbols. I find this problematic.

Subjective Versus Objective Interpretation

Jung feels that everything in a dream can be interpreted in two ways. Let's say you dream of your cousin, who in the dream acts like a clown. An interpretation on the objective level would look at your dream for what it would tell you about your actual cousin – your feelings and perceptions of him. Your dream might help you take your cousin more seriously, by seeing beneath his clownish exterior. Or if you were thinking of taking him into your business, it might be warning you he is not suitable partnership material.

On the other hand, an interpretation on the subjective level would see your cousin as an aspect of your own personality. You'd think about the clownish aspects of yourself – perhaps the evening before you were uneasy in a social situation and played the clown in order to conceal this. The dream might help you understand this better. This would be an interpretation on the subjective level.

It is worth getting a sense now of how these different kinds of interpretation can lead to very different understandings of a dream. Try the exercise on page 60.

Active Imagination

Jung would encourage patients to engage with dream symbols through the use of *active imagination*. This is a kind of meditation, in which you evoke an image or symbol from a dream, feel its life, and then see how it developed in your imagination. Jung also used a wide variety of methods to express and elaborate his own dreams and visions, including working with clay, sculpture, and drawing pictures and mandalas. All these are very useful ways of engaging with your dream world, and I'll talk more about them in the section on dream work.

Jung's Importance

For me, Jung's importance is in how he expands our conception of dreams, and the methods we can use to illuminate them. His emphasis on elucidating the real world of the dreamer as the context for a particular dream, his notions of subjective and objective interpretation, compensation and of the way dreams can contribute to human growth, all have changed the landscape of dream work. The notion of archetypes has become part of our language.

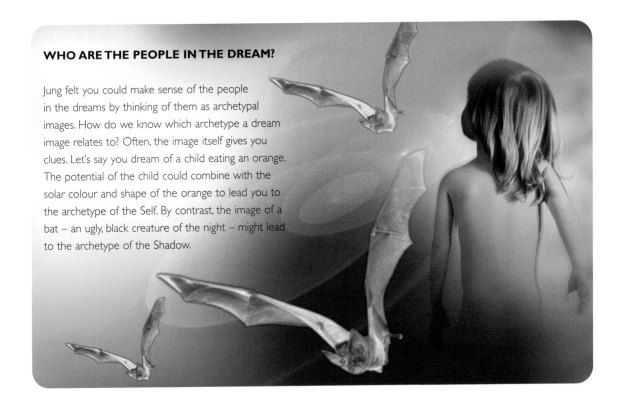

WHO ARE THE PEOPLE IN THE DREAM?

Jung felt you could make sense of the people in the dreams by thinking of them as archetypal images. How do we know which archetype a dream image relates to? Often, the image itself gives you clues. Let's say you dream of a child eating an orange. The potential of the child could combine with the solar colour and shape of the orange to lead you to the archetype of the Self. By contrast, the image of a bat – an ugly, black creature of the night – might lead to the archetype of the Shadow.

Your Nightly Dream Theatre

Jung pointed out that every dream has a dramatic structure, much like that of the classical Greek drama described by Aristotle. The advantage of looking at dreams in this way is that it highlights the way the plot helps carry the dream's message.

Take a dream and look at the following:

1   **Place, time, dramatis personae**
    All these are generally defined at the beginning of the dream. Each sets the dream in a particular personal and psychic location. Where is your dream situated?

2   **Exposition**
    The background information necessary to appreciate the drama. This helps define the question the dream poses. In cinema terms, this is the back story – what has happened *before* the dream started?

3   **Peripety**
    The change in fortune or reversal of circumstances that set the story in motion. The old writer's guideline (very loosely translated from Aristotle) Act one: Get your hero up in a tree. Act two: Throw rocks at your hero (make his life even more difficult). Act Three: Get your hero down from the tree. Getting your hero up in a tree is the peripety. What is the tree you are up?

4   **Resolution**
    Acts two and three. The solution of the problem posed in the exposition, usually with some accompanying learning. For Jung, the resolution discloses the compensatory message of the dream. How is the dream resolved?

James Hillman

James Hillman (*The Dream and the Underworld*) and Patricia Berry call themselves archetypal psychologists and I include them here because they question many of our basic assumptions about dream work.

Everyone who works with dreams has three experiences that Hillman explores. First we feel a sense of depth. This is hard to define, yet tangible for all who work with and listen to dreams. We feel we are going deeper, discovering something under the surface of our ordinary lives. We sense we are making a connection with a part of ourselves that is often ignored. This is part of why dream work is so satisfying. Freud and Jung called this deeper part of ourselves the "unconscious". Hillman calls it an experience of "soul".

Along with this sense of depth is a sense of initiation. However determinedly practical our approach to dreams, we have a sense that they – and our work with them – introduce us to something new, a new world of images and new ways of being. Hillman calls this the "underworld", and he links this to the mythological understandings of the realm of Hades.

Finally, when we work with dreams – either one-to-one or in groups – we have the sense of being cared for, as if our dreams are looking out for us, helping us in the ways they can, keeping us "in mind", a bit like our parents did when we were young. Hillman calls this sense "imaginal love".

Dreams as Poetry

For Hillman, dreams are first and foremost products of our imagination. They are like poetry. Their being and life is fragile. We all remember "analyzing" poems at school. When we were finished with this often tedious task, our sense of the poem's magic was gone. We had an "interpretation" but no poetry.

Much work with dreams makes a similar error – it aims to replace the dream with an interpretation, practical advice or a prediction about the future. In all this, we quickly move away from the mystery and life of the dream, its power to move and affect us in ways we don't understand.

It's not that we can't learn from dreams – although Hillman sometimes seems to question even this. It's more that any dream work we do should leave the dream's "life" intact, so that we preserve a sense of it as a glimpse of a different world that we do not fully understand.

In doing this, we preserve the power of our dreams to continue to affect us, to return in our thoughts, to colour our days. Often, compelling dreams keep this power for months and even years. Not all dreams – or poetry for that matter – have quite this capacity, but they all have a life we can treasure.

The work of a dream, according to Hillman and one of his co-theorists, Patricia Berry, is to digest the perceptions, experiences and "material" of the day, and to turn it into images. This is important because for them images are the food of the soul. Think of the way you can feel nourished by reading poetry. The images, the connections, the language and rhythm of the poem, all feed a deep part of ourselves.

For Hillman, dreams are first and foremost products of our imagination.

> *We can approach dream work to learn, or we can approach it to take.*

If after working with a dream all you can remember is your interpretation, you've not kept its spirit alive and you've destroyed the way it is "soul food".

The "Heroic" Ego

If our aim is to conserve the life of the dream, the spirit with which we approach it matters greatly. We can approach dream work to learn, or we can approach it to take.

For Hillman, much of our work with dreams is a manifestation of the "heroic ego". Like Hercules when he descended into Hades, we enter the world of the dream and dream work with a lack of recognition of its difference from the day-world and a determination to master this new territory. In this spirit, Freud called himself a "conquistador". The conquistadors didn't see the beauty and value of the art of the Aztecs and Incas. They only saw that it was made of gold which, when melted down, would make them rich. When we approach dreams as conquistadors, we make the same mistake. We don't see the beauty and value of the dream world, we only aim to profit from it by extracting what lessons we can and then moving on. Think of how the

rainforests, so rich in as yet undiscovered flora and fauna, are being levelled by farmers and loggers who want to profit from their wood and soil. They see only a short-term gain, and not the long-term costs. When we are dream conquistadors, we follow in these footsteps. We become the worst kind of dream capitalists.

We can learn an enormous amount from our dreams, but one of their most important lessons is in helping us practice a different, gentler approach in which we learn from the world, and don't "put nature on the rack".

Dream Conservation

If we are not to level the dream rainforest to profit from it, how can we approach it?

For Hillman, the golden rule is to keep the dream alive, "dream work is conservation". If we look at how dreams work in healing cults and religious mysteries, we see that the dreams themselves change the participants, even to the extent of healing profound physical problems. It's not what is made of the dream afterwards, but the experience of the dream while dreaming *and* afterwards, that makes a difference.

When a dream is experienced as being given by gods or spirits, its power is increased enormously. For us, I believe the profoundest experience of the dream does not come just from the experience of the dream alone, but also from our work with it, which helps us realize its depth and wisdom.

Dream Characters

Perhaps one of the ways we can easily see the distinctiveness of Hillman's approach is in the way he understands dream characters, and in particular the dream ego.

Hillman believes that dream characters are best understood as *daimones* – heroes and gods who appear to us in the shape of people we know in dreams. In other words, every dream character, however ordinary and literal they might seem to us – our tyrannical boss, our jealous sister, our gossipy neighbour – has an archetypal element. Our dream characters represent both our personal traits (the way we can be tyrannical, jealous and gossipy) and divine traits.

To deal with the subjective level – the way our dream characters show us our personal traits – we *take back projections*. We look for the way our dream characters show us aspects of ourselves. We reflect on the way we are tyrannical, jealous and gossipy. But we do not do this in a moralistic way – "I should be less possessive", or "I should keep my big mouth shut". Rather we see the way we are mirrored in our dream characters, they show us our own potentials.

But not just our own characteristics. Our dream characters also help us access an archetypal reality. The way we can get a sense of this is to capitalize our descriptions – "The-Boss-Who-Is-Tyrannical", "My-Sister-Who-Is-Jealous", "The-Neighbour-Who-Knows-Everybody's-Business".

When we do this, we realize our dream characters are larger than life, they are gods cloaked in human forms. The Greek legends are full of gods who assumed a human form for one reason or another. We can get a whiff of this every night in our dreams.

Capitalizing our characters' names in this way helps us see the power and the ubiquity of those "personal" traits we are more likely to judge than embrace. The Greek gods were jealous, tyrannical, mischievous and worse. They legitimized these experiences for us – if the gods could behave this way, so could we.

Our dream characters are not literal people – though they may indeed be people we have had contact with in the day. But we never dream of these people literally – they are always different. They wear a different expression, clothes, or appear in a different context. In these minor transformations, we are already starting to "digest" them, to bring out their subjective meaning for us and their archetypal characteristics, making them into food for our reflections and soul.

You can also use the same technique to get a larger-than-life sense of actions in dreams – "The Cousin Who Puts You Down", "The Girl Who Teases And Flirts Dangerously", "The Soldier Who Kills Everyone In Sight". Why not try capitalizing the characters and actions in a recent dream of yours?

The Rightness of the Dream

When we have a dream we don't understand, it's easy to make judgments based on our pre-existing understanding of ourselves, and to project them into the dreams. It's much more difficult to see and stay with the rightness of the dream.

Patricia Berry says that the dream is "just-so" and that its truth is precisely articulated. An attitude that helps you see this is "when-then". John's dream:

I'm telling my father about a successful presentation at work. He said he'd just made a deal worth 10 million.

When John begins to feel successful, then his father puts his "success" into the shade. Each response is a condition of the other. This way of seeing the dream takes it away from being a general commentary on your life, and brings out your involvement in a particular "tango". To understand this tango better, you'd go into it in greater depth, through reflecting on both partners' steps and how they occasion one another.

HILLMAN ON WATER IN DREAMS

Entering into water relaxes our hold on things and enables us to let go where we have been stuck – think of the effect of a hot bath when your body is stiff and sore. In this sense, water in a dream can be a new environment, belief-system or relationship – in which our old rigidities dissolve. The soul loves water for this reason – it hates the ego's certainties.

Water can be different temperatures – cold, hot, warm – and have different visual characteristics – clear, muddy, reflective. It can be deep or shallow. It may flow, sit or rush.

While water is often interpreted as emotions or the unconscious, there is much more depth in immersing oneself in the particular water it is.

Medard Boss

Once upon a time, I, Chang-Tsu, dreamt I was a butterfly, fluttering hither and thither. I was aware only of following my fancy as a butterfly. Suddenly I awoke, and there I lay, myself again. Now I do not know whether I was a man dreaming I was a butterfly, or whether I am a butterfly dreaming I am a man.

Chang-Tsu, a chinese philosopher and follower of Lao-Tsu, points here to the reality of our experience of dreaming. At every moment in a dream, we find ourselves in a world. We react to what happens in a way that makes sense to us and is shaped by our mood in the moment. All this is exactly the same as when we're awake.

We can have dreams where we do pretty much everything we can when we're awake. We can:

- Experience a frightening, or friendly, world
- Have an argument and resolve it, or not
- Make love, or avoid making love
- Have spiritual experiences
- Think reflectively
- Be critical about what we and others think
- Wake up
- Wake up and then remember a dream
- Wake up, remember, and then interpret a dream

Medard Boss, a follower of the philosopher Martin Heidegger, is different from our other dream theorists in that he approaches dreams from a philosophical point of view rather than a scientific one. He emphasizes that our experience of being in a dream is simply another way of being in the world, much closer in essence to waking reality than we usually think. He would suggest that we can learn most from our dreams by actually sticking with the dream experience.

Most of us follow Freud and Jung in doing precisely the opposite, often in spite of our best intentions. Why is this? Because most of us have been deeply inculcated with the assumptions of a scientific attitude.

our experience of being in a dream is simply another way of being in the world, much closer in essence to waking reality than we usually think.

Boss argues that our scientific way of seeing things impoverishes our experience of the world and our capacity to learn from it. And working with dreams is a way to remedy this impoverishment.

Surface and Depth

We have come to believe that the truth of things lies underneath or behind the surface. Like Freud, we assume that, "perceived phenomena must give way to the assumed interplay of drives and impulses". We leave what we perceive behind, and try to get under the surface of things. This makes the "surface" thin and meaningless.

For Freud, what was underneath the dream were the unconscious, repressed wishes and the mechanisms of condensation and displacement. For Jung, what was underneath the dream were archetypes, a complicated structure of the psyche, and various functions such as compensation. Both end up talking much more about what they assume is underneath or behind the dream (the dream work, the structure of the psyche) than what actually happens in it. They both argue that what they are assuming is underneath the dream is really true.

Even Hillman, who in many ways is similar to Boss in his approach, quickly moves away from the dream as dreamed to the dream as envisioned in the underworld.

So Boss's approach is radical. He argues that our scientific way of seeing things impoverishes our experience of the world and our capacity to learn from it. And working with dreams is a way to remedy this impoverishment.

Both Boss and Heidegger want us to stick with the phenomena – what we experience – of human life. They follow Goethe. As he wrote, "Don't look for anything behind phenomena, they themselves are the lesson".

When you look at the way we are whether awake or dreaming, several things become apparent. We ex-ist, from the Latin to stand out [ex + sistere]. For Boss, Heidegger and the phenomenologists, we stand out into Being. This points to the way we are not in our heads (as science would have it) but out there in-the-world. Our experience – whether writing a book, washing dishes, playing football or reading to a child – is that we are involved in whatever we are doing. We are equally involved when we are "just" feeling. When we are angry with someone, our experience is that we are *in* the argument, whether we're having it in our head or in the world. The world in which we stand out, in which we ex-ist, is full of meaning for us, whether awake or dreaming.

Time and Space

Boss argues that the way we experience time and space in dreams is closer to our lived experience than the scientific understanding of time and space we have learned.

Think about physical closeness to others in dreams. In dreams we experience being physically close to people who are "in reality" distant in space (they live far away) or time (they may have passed on). Boss argues that the physical closeness in our dreams mirrors our emotional reality. So when we are close to someone in a dream, it indicates our emotional closeness, and it mirrors the way we feel there is no distance between us and the ones we love. This is a truer experiential reality than the distance or time that separates us.

Time too is very different in our experience than the clock time of seconds, minutes and hours. When we are involved with something or someone, time flies. When we are bored (a narrowing of attention in which we are uninvolved with anything), time crawls. Our primary experience of time is that we have time for someone or something, or not. This is what is mirrored in a dream.

It's also true that we "travel through time" much more when we're awake than we normally think. If we pay attention to our thoughts from moment to moment, we see how one moment we're in the future – thinking of how we'll spend our big lottery win, the next we're in the past – mulling over our boss's sarcastic comment when we arrived at work late, and the next we're in the present, enjoying the taste of our morning coffee. Our experience of time from moment to moment is much more like the way time jumps around in dreams than we usually think.

Our True Possibilities

When we are awake, the world that occupies us is that of external realities (which may mean little or nothing to us) and the ways in which we try to "fit in" with what is expected of us.

In dreams we are cut off from these external realities. So we can dream only of what we are truly open to, whether this be joy, fear or anxiety. In dreams, we can see what matters to us and how we see the world. This makes dream work a privileged way of having access to our hearts and true selves.

Mood

Along with our primary experience of time and space, dreams bring us into contact with the importance of mood in shaping our experience of reality. Our mood – whether dreaming or waking – determines those possibilities we can see in the world.

When we're depressed, the world presents us with few positive prospects. The world looks grey and prospectless, and we feel down. In our experience, depression comes at us, so to speak, from the world. Similarly, when people we don't know look welcoming and friendly, we feel happy.

In our dreams, we see the power of our moods to evoke memories and realities. When we're joyous, we find things associated with great joy in our dreams – even things we'd long since forgotten. Childhood moments, that menu from the hotel during our honeymoon, fragments of songs. The same is true when we are fearful – our fear evokes a frightening world drawing on frightening events from our past. What is so interesting in dreams is how quickly one mood can follow another, completely changing the dream landscape. But isn't this also what we're like when we're awake?

Two Questions

So Boss dispenses with all the apparatus of the scientific study of dreams – the unconscious mind, the self, the ego, the psyche, wish fulfilment, collective unconscious – and replaces it with a different understanding of what dreams are, simply another way of being-in-the-world.

The importance of dreams is that they show us what we are truly open to and our true possibilities – what matters to us.

To get access to what the dream tells us about this, Boss asks two simple questions of each dream:
- To what possibilities is the dreamer so open that they have entered his dream world?
- How does the dreamer respond to what is revealed to him in his dream? In particular, what mood or emotional attunement shapes this response?

The first question asks, what happens in your dreams? (And conversely, what never happens? Do you never make love, experience a lovely meal, argue, or fight?) The second, how do you respond?

I'll flesh out the power of these questions in the next chapter.

5

Dreams and
Our World

Dream Possibilities

Dreams show us how we see and construct the world. This was something I learned from a class I ran in 1975. The class was held during the day at an innovative adult education institute in London. For the purposes of the education authority, we were a dream class, in which I would talk about different theories of dreams. But the people who ran the institute, most of whom attended the class, were interested in something more experiential.

To please everyone, I'd do a short 20-minute lecture on some aspect of dream theory or research, then we'd use the rest of the time for a dream sharing group. I'd recently discovered Kilton Stewart's writings on the Senoi (see page 112) and was keen to see what would develop out of a group of people meeting regularly to share dreams.

The class had an unusual composition. The majority of members were mothers getting time off during the day, but the class also included most of the institute staff and a biker (Roger) who happened to be interested in dreams. Each class, we sat in a circle and went around sharing our dreams of the week before. We did this for 24 weeks. Over this time, we made two major discoveries.

Usually in the mothers' dreams there were children; they were in trouble, and the mothers would do anything, including sacrifice their lives, to save them. At the other end of the scale were Roger's dreams. Every week it was another scene of battle or devastation. In Roger's dreams, the rule was kill or be killed. There were corpses, enemies and weapons, but never – except towards the end of the group – a helping hand.

These different night worlds mirrored the different day worlds the two groups inhabited. The mothers lived in a world shaped by their love and concern for their children; Roger lived in a world where he felt nobody could be trusted, nothing was safe, everything was a battle.

Roger had dreamed this way for as long as he could remember. When we first went around the circle telling our dreams, he literally couldn't believe that other people dreamed differently. He thought the mothers had made their dreams up. "I could never have dreamed that!" he said. The mothers, on their side, were shocked by *his* night world. They couldn't imagine what it would be like to dream of a post-nuclear holocaust every night.

When Roger was awake, he could always find evidence for his world view — that people were really out to get him. So it didn't surprise him that he dreamed this way every night. That was the way the world was, after all!

What made him question this was that the others clearly didn't experience, or dream of, the world this way. Nor did the class treat him like an enemy. After a long period of resistance – he first thought the mothers (and me) were trying to con him and he dismissed us all as hopelessly naïve – he began to reflect on the way he saw the world in his dreams.

He began to question that he dreamed this way because the world *was* this way, and began to see that this was how *he saw* the world, the way he construed it. In other words, he made a major developmental shift. He realized that the world he experienced in his dreams and waking life was a world he had constructed. He began to see there was no inevitability about this and that his world view could change. Of course, this is crucially important, because as our view of the world changes, so does our daily reality.

New possibilities began to appear in his dreams. I remember how we all laughed when, for the first time, someone gave him a helping hand in a dream – it was a motherly woman who gave him a gun he needed for yet another dream showdown. This, however, represented a breakthrough. It was a new possibility of relationship – not just kill or be killed – but someone helping him with no ulterior motive.

Of course, Roger was an extreme case – his dreams only embodied one possible world. Most of us have a much wider range of possibilities in dreams. And yet, some scenarios will predominate. We'll engage with the world anxiously because the world always has the potential to harm us emotionally or physically. We'll regularly feel excluded from whatever is going on. Or we'll be constantly frustrated in our attempts to accomplish our goals. (In one recent dream group, a woman had a series of dreams where she just couldn't get anything she wanted to eat – she'd be fighting to get through a crowd to get to a suitcase of food especially prepared for her, or she wouldn't be able to find the flavour of ice cream she wanted, or she'd be eating in a Japanese restaurant where the chopsticks wouldn't hold the food.)

Certain things will happen in our dreams, and other things won't. Some people never have a chance to consummate a love relationship. Some shy away from confrontations. Still others never cry, laugh or experience ecstatic happiness.

We can experience infinite possibilities in our lives, but most of us live within a much more limited world, a world we construct from moment to moment. As much the same thing happens from day to day, most of us, like Roger, come to believe that this is the "real world". We wonder at those others who seem to experience different possibilities.

We can always find validation for how we see the world. (If we are paranoid, like Roger, we see what we take to be the little disguised signs of people's hostility everywhere.) So we are caught in a circle – we expect to see the real world in a certain way, and that's how we find it. If our early experience taught us that people aren't to be trusted and are out to harm us, we always eventually find this in the people we meet later. If our early experience is that

A NEUROCOGNITIVE THEORY OF DREAMS

G. William Domhoff, a research psychologist and author of several books on dreams, reminds us that:

- Dreaming depends on the normal functioning of a neural network in the brain. This network is primarily involved in the way we construct an internal representation of the world.

- When you study children's dreams, you find that they don't dream as often as adults and that their dreams develop in complexity with age. Only six percent of REM awakenings produce dreams at age six; 39 percent at 12. Up to the age of five, children's dreams tend to be of single images – an animal or something to eat. From five to eight, a simple narrative (a few actions and characters) develops. It is only between ages 13–15 that children's dreams become as long and as complex as adults'. This parallels the development of their brains and their increasing mastery of language.

- Analysis of the content of dreams shows that they reflect similar concerns and emotions to those that dominate our waking lives.

Domhoff argues that this evidence points to the fact that dreaming is best understood as a developmental cognitive achievement, which mirrors our perception of the world.

people love and respect us, we confirm this in our later experiences. Partly this happens because we are unconsciously drawn to people and situations that will confirm our basic beliefs. And partly it happens because we subtly (and unconsciously) act on people and situations until they are like we always knew they would be.

As long as we're awake, we can always find evidence for our world-view. But when we're

*Dreams show us our
world construction
"software" in action.*

dreaming, we find ourselves in the same safe, unsafe, anxiety-causing, happy or terrifying world. We can't argue that this is the outside world. It must be the world as we see it. Dreams show us our world construction "software" in action. They give us the chance to "own" how we see the world.

Seeing dreams as showing us how we create our world is enormously powerful in itself. But dreams don't just show us how we construct the world. Dreams can give us the first signs that our way of seeing the world is changing. We can have new experiences in dreams. Roger was given a helping hand, others find themselves having the first inkling of a relationship with a woman/man in a dream. Some people sob for the first time in a dream, and still others experience joy for the first time. Often, new behaviours appear first in a dream, and then begin to happen in daily life. These new behaviours may appear in the dream "you", or perhaps in some other character.

CHANGE ON THE WAY

A rough way of seeing how "close" you are to embodying the new possibility is to gauge your distance from the character in the dream who displays it. If it's a close friend, you are "close" to the new behaviour, if a stranger, more distant. But in any case, the fact that a new possibility appears in your dream means its now "in" your world.

Software and Language

When we talk about software being involved in the construction of our world, we're also talking about language. In our dreams, as in our waking world, we experience the enormous power of language in shaping our world. (Indeed, Heidegger and others argue that we couldn't have the experience of a world without language.)

Expressions, metaphor, simile, exaggeration, opposites and word play are all embodied in dreams, often in a very literal sense. (We feel/are low, blue, high or small; we turn into a hyena while laughing.) These mechanisms of language also shape our experience of the waking world.

Dreams in Dialogue

The second discovery we made in this dream class was a result of the unusual way we'd scheduled the group. Every week we'd have a talk on some dream theorist, and every week everyone in the group would share a dream from the previous week. I'd talk about theorists who everybody knew (or at least had heard of) like Freud and Jung, and other theorists who were relatively unknown, such as Hillman, Boss and, most obscurely, Francis Mott – a man who believes all dreams reflect experiences inside the womb. Given that I had only 20 minutes, I'd be talking about each thinker over a number of weeks.

We were all struck by the way that what people dreamed from week to week was influenced by the dream theorists being talked about. The group's dream imagery and content literally changed so that it fit the model of the theorist of the week. Phallic symbols and disguised wish-fulfilments would appear during the weeks I talked about Freud, archetypal images when I talked about Jung, and twisting three-stranded umbilical cords when I talked about Mott.

There is other anecdotal evidence for this idea; people who go from Jungian to Freudian therapy – or vice versa – find their dreams change to reflect the language of their therapists.

We were able to see, week by week, the truths that each theorist had found and believed were

GENERAL EXPERIMENTER EFFECTS

If you like, I'm arguing that dreams are part of a well-known effect in psychology, the experimenter effect. If you tell an experimenter to expect certain results from the study she is doing, she somehow produces the results she expected. This happens even if you make it clear to the experimenter she mustn't communicate her expectation to the experimental subjects, and you restrict the experimenter's interaction to simply reading instructions from a piece of paper. This well-known effect is very much like what happens in therapy and dream groups.

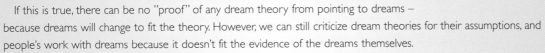

The therapist or group leader expects to get a certain kind of dream, but doesn't communicate it to his clients because that would "distort the results". But the client has non-verbal ways of finding out what is expected, and produces dreams to order. One such non-verbal technique – of watching the experimenter's eyes to find out what he really wants and feels – is developed by babies as early as one year old.

If this is true, there can be no "proof" of any dream theory from pointing to dreams – because dreams will change to fit the theory. However, we can still criticize dream theories for their assumptions, and people's work with dreams because it doesn't fit the evidence of the dreams themselves.

universal. I am convinced it is this phenomena that convinces any dream theorist he or she is on the right track. Jung expected to find archetypal images in dreams, and he found more and more, proving he was right. Freud, too, found what he was looking for and I can only assume it's true for me, too.

What sense can we make of this? For me, it shows how remembering and working with dreams is a project in which your dreams are active partners. Earlier, when I talked about keeping a dream diary, I used the metaphor of dreams as a person who you'd like to get to know, and said that he or she responded to your interest. As you get to know someone better, they begin to speak your language – so that they can communicate better with you.

In the dream class, our project was to discover the meaning of dreams and dream theories together. And what better way to do this than by example! Our dreams became an active partner in the conversation.

If there is any single message to this book, it is this – that dreams will cooperate with you in almost any project you want them to. In the section about Solution Dreams (see pages 32–41), you saw how responsive dreams were to a request or challenge. The same is true for almost any request you might have – to have lucid dreams, psychic dreams, Hillmanian dreams, whatever. You can have an ongoing dialogue with your dreams, as with a friend.

The Moral Labyrinth

"To err is human, to forgive divine." As a definition of what it is to be human, I find this quote from Alexander Pope difficult to beat. To be human is to err, to get things wrong. When we get things wrong, when we act inappropriately, when we mess up, that's when we're most human. What we aim for (at our best) is to forgive ourselves and others for these human errors. In this, we find our highest humanity, our divinity, our wholeness.

Dream Baggage

Working with dreams can help us in this quest. But first we need to discard some heavy and unwanted baggage. I'm talking about our propensity to judge first and think later. Moral judgments come easily to us. "How naïve she was to trust him." "Does he ever think before he leaps?" "He's so greedy." And so on. It's difficult for us not to think in terms of right/wrong, good/bad and praise/blame.

The Greek word hamartia, *usually translated as "sin" in the New Testament, is an archery term that literally means "to miss the mark", "to miss the target".*

We don't escape these judgments when we dream, and when we reflect on our dreaming. When you dream of eating the food out of your baby's mouth, your first thought on waking (and sometimes in the dream) is, "I shouldn't do this. It's wrong." And maybe "what would people think of me if they knew I'd dreamed that?"

I'm not arguing that stealing food out of your baby's mouth is good practice, to be hailed and praised. Rather, I'm saying that immediately judging yourself is not the best way to get to the heart of your dream.

Missing the Mark

A brief digression: The Greek word *hamartia*, usually translated as "sin" in the New Testament, is an archery term that literally means "to miss the mark", "to miss the target".

I understand this word very much in the light of Alexander Pope's definition. To sin, to miss the target, is to be human. Dreams show us missing the target (and sometimes hitting it) much as we do in life. Missing the target is not properly an occasion for judgment – you're wrong/bad/blameworthy. Rather, it should make you reflect, much as when you miss the target in an archery competition. Questions like "Did you adequately correct for the wind, distance and your wonky shoulder?" and "How were you distracted?" will help you get closer to the target with your next arrow. Questions like "How did you miss that easy shot, you moron?" or "Are you totally hopeless, you clumsy oaf?" won't.

Which questions are more familiar to you? For most of us, it's the latter. Many of us go around telling ourselves how stupid, inadequate, weak and useless we are. It's too easy to repeat this error with dreams, to see dreams as a rich source of material to increase our perceived inadequacies.

Why do we speak to ourselves so harshly? For some of us, it reflects how we were spoken to when young. But even children who grow up with parents who wouldn't dream of speaking to them in such tones can have inner voices more akin to a slave master than a helpful friend.

Dreams don't tell us what to do, or what we should do. They tell us what we are doing, how we see things, what we want.

Some people defend this way of speaking to themselves – they say it enables them to learn. In their minds, condemning children is obviously the best way to teach them to grow up to be responsible, caring adults.

Not Knowing

Most of us, including me, don't have a clue what a dream means when we first dream/hear it. We're not keen on not having a clue. We'd prefer to be in the place of the one who knows. Making a judgment is a shortcut to knowing. You may not know what the dream is about, but you know greed is wrong. Suddenly, you feel both better and worse. Better because as the judger, as the moral arbiter, you know what's right. Worse, because this knowing is at the expense of the part of you that feels, and also at the cost of the truth of the dream.

Moral judgment, this easy way of making ourselves feel righteous, destroys our capacity to reflect, ask questions, and learn from our dreams. It is the enemy of the reflection that allows you to see your error, correct your aim, reduce, if you will, your sin. It is the baggage we need to put down before we can work with dreams freely.

We all dream of things we wouldn't imagine doing when awake. We're greedy, covetous, aggressive, thoughtless. We err in different, and often more dramatic, ways than we would permit in our waking lives. If we can accept these human failings, we can make links to those aspects of ourselves that in our usual self-judgment we expunge from our consciousness. We can see, and forgive, those aspects of ourselves we judge out of existence. In accepting our errors in dreaming, as when awake, we get closer to the divine, or being whole.

Negative Capability

Keats called the capacity to bear "uncertainties, mysteries, [and] doubts without any irritable reaching after fact and reason" (and we might add moral judgment) *negative capability*. He felt it was this quality that enabled an individual to become what he called a "Man of Achievement". He had Shakespeare in mind. Literature and poetry are close bedfellows. And, as we will see, the creative use of language in dreams has many similarities with poetry.

I'm not sure we want to become Men/Women of Achievement in relation to dreams, but I know that doing dream work requires the ability to bear the uncertainties, mysteries and doubts of hearing and having dreams of which, initially, we can't make any sense of at all.

No "Should" in Dreams

Dreams don't tell us what to do, or what we should do. They tell us what we are doing, how we see things, what we want. But if we see what we want and what we're doing, we are in a better position to act and to know what we should do. This is important because otherwise we can deny our moral responsibility by saying "my dream told me to do it". You can take advice from dreams, as from anyone who knows you well, but it's best to reserve your ultimate decisions about action for yourself. A dream may show you how unhappy you are in a relationship, but it can't show you that you should end the relationship. And this is a decision that shouldn't just be taken on the basis of a dream, but on reflecting on what the dream has shown you together with all the other things you know.

Seeing how unhappy we are in a relationship can make us realize we need to address the difficulties. A dream may also clarify what's bothering us (as did James's Solution Dream) and what's important for us to address.

Dreams as a Playground

Dreams are like a world-sized playground in which you can experiment with ways of being and allow yourself to think, feel, and do things you couldn't otherwise entertain. You can play house, doctor, lover, husband, wife, cop or robber. Like children who discover so much in these games, you can learn from all of this, reflecting on how it shows you what works for you and what doesn't. What stops you from playing and learning is premature moral judgment.

It may be too much to ask that we stop exercising our judgment reflexes when working with dreams. Maybe the best we can hope for is to move our righteous selves from centre stage. Then, we can allow ourselves to be who we are, and acknowledge the thoughts and feelings of which we seem capable. When we do this, we don't condemn ourselves for our playground politics, rather, we rejoice in the full panoply of our humanity, good and bad. We leave the moral labyrinth and create the best conditions for learning from our dreams, for getting the most from our human errors.

Right Attitude and Right Mindfulness

We're now ready to set aside our moral judgments and to play in our night-world playground. What else is involved in having the right attitude to dreams and dream work? In the section on Hillman, I outlined a couple of other necessary basic components. They are: respect for the dream, come to the dream to learn and not to take and, above all, keep the dream alive.

Respect for the Dream

When you talk to someone for the first time, much more can happen if you approach the person with respect – respect for what he or she has to say and for his or her point of view. Respect this person's otherness. The same is true for dreams. You'll get more out of your dialogue with them if you assume your dream has something important to say to you.

Your respect for your dreams will develop as you work with them. You'll come to see they mean exactly what they say, and say exactly what they mean. You'll realize that even what seemed to be extraneous has an important role in conveying the dream's message.

Come to the Dream to Learn

Humility is one of the virtues modernity doesn't have much time for. We feel we have to know everything, and the two things people find hardest to say are "I don't know", and "I was wrong".

At the start of our dream work we usually have to say "I don't know (what this dream is about)". And by the end, we often have to say, "I got this wrong (in some way)". These can feel like difficult pills to swallow.

As long as we recognize we don't know everything and that to err is human, we have the right attitude and can learn from our dreams.

The other side of this is that we don't come to dreams only to take. Dream work isn't a one-night stand. There may be insights we can take away from our work with dreams, even in a night, but truly, our insight develops over a period of time as we get to know our dreams better.

Keep the Dream Alive

This really is simple – we don't want to replace the lively vivid spirit of the dream with a dead interpretation. Ideally, when we finish our work, our dream is still alive and our appreciation of it and its messages has increased. This way the dream can continue to work on us through time.

You Know Best

Part of what has given dream work (and psychotherapy) a bad name, is the idea that the therapist always knows best, that someone else can know your dream better than you, and that your disagreement with their interpretation can simply be dismissed as "resistance". All this is, of course, nonsense.

You are the best person to judge whether an interpretation of your dream makes sense. How do you know? Part of the answer is that it rings a bell, it clicks, it feels right. This is subjective, but not *just* subjective.

That's because all these expressions actually point towards something rather profound. A correct interpretation brings something into focus. You see something you didn't see before. You recognize a

when you've had a chance to process the interpretation. Sometimes it happens with an image in the dream, sometimes with the dream as a whole.

Suspicious Clicks

Dreams don't show up to tell you what you already know. So you should always be suspicious of "clicks" that simply confirm what you think already. If you know you're anxious, you don't need a dream to tell you that. If you know you're unhappy at work, or that your boss is a tyrant, you should be suspicious of interpretations that simply affirm this. There is probably more to the dream than these comforting clicks would indicate.

Evidence

How can you tell the difference between a truthful click and a suspicious one? A simple way is that a truthful click will tell you something new, or will make you realize something emotionally which you have recognized before but only intellectually.

A suspicious click often fits one part of the dream but ignores others. A truthful click accords with the evidence of the dream (and our associations). A suspicious click doesn't.

I'm not using evidence in the legal sense, but in its wider sense of "a thing or things helpful in forming a conclusion or judgment". It's not enough for a dream interpretation to feel right. That's because we all have a profound capacity for self-deception, and are likely to exercise it most powerfully when we are under the influence of one dream theory or another. We need to check our conclusions against the evidence of the dream as a whole. When we do this, we find some of our clicks are validated and others are brought into question (see the box for a couple of examples).

Looking at the evidence is an aspect of respect for the dream. If we assume a dream means what it says, we shouldn't twist it to make our interpretations work. Even if we're very attached to our interpretation …

truth because it makes sense of a number of facts that previously seemed disparate and unconnected.

Think of the *Star Wars* trilogy. Halfway through the second episode (of the original three), Darth Vader and Luke Skywalker are having a fight to the death. Vader says to Luke – "I'm your father." As he says this, our minds (and presumably Luke's) flash back to all the incidents in the previous movies that now make sense in the light of this new fact (interpretation). This is an example of how a good interpretation works – what Vader says "clicks" for Luke (and us) because it brings the world into a different focus, and makes sense of facts that previously seemed unconnected.

The Greek word for truth is *alietheia*, literally un-hiddenness. In other words, truth is bringing something from darkness (hiddenness) into the light. If an interpretation makes something "click" for you, it's because it shows you something that was previously hidden or unconscious. In other words, the feeling that an interpretation rings a bell, clicks, or just feels right points to no less than a shining out of truth.

Sometimes this "click" happens when you're working with a dream, sometimes a day or two later. Sometimes when somebody has suggested an interpretation of the dream, and sometimes only

CHECKING OUT CLICKS

Helen, a woman in a recent dream group, had the following fragment of a dream:

"I was having a warm affectionate hug with a man. I pulled away, still feeling the warmth. Then I realized I'd lost an earring – at this, I lost the warm feeling of the connection and the hug."

In the dream group we'd been exploring Helen's difficulty is sustaining intimacy with a man. Here, she is having an intimate moment, but breaks it. The pulling away and the loss of the earring flesh out her difficulty. They are in the dream to tell us the whys and wherefores of her difficulty in sustaining intimacy (and, perhaps especially, physical intimacy).

Helen's main association to the dream was to an incident with her father when she was seven or eight. They'd been extremely close; he had been an ally in her regular battles with her mother. But on this occasion her mother had demanded that her father punish her for something that had happened earlier in the day. Her father had come to her room and had told her not to do it again. He was going to leave, when her mother demanded repeatedly he do more – and, to get his wife off his back, he had ended up hitting Helen again and again, saying "I hope this satisfies her." Helen hadn't spoken for several days afterwards and had vowed she would never let anyone touch her again.

Helen remembered this incident with much feeling. Clearly it was an important memory that had a bearing on her difficulty sustaining intimacy with a man, but was it really linked with the dream? I wanted confirmation.

Earlier, when associating to the dream, she had told us that the earrings had been purchased in Japan. I asked again about the earrings (I wanted to know whether they had a connection with her father, which would confirm her association). Helen said she had bought the earrings the first Christmas after her father died. She couldn't bear to go home, so she had flown to Australia. She bought the earrings at a stopover in Japan, on Christmas Day. She had worn them constantly for 15 years.

This association clearly links the earrings to her father – they were a present to herself, a replacement for his loss. It thus provides evidence for the association that links her father to the man in the dream.

An example of how evidence can bring a dream interpretation into question came from Isabelle. She told this dream:

"I was in a desolate place. Everyone around was dead. I saw two policemen. I wasn't sure they were alive so I touched their clothes. They were alive and they confirmed I was too. I felt very pleased and relieved."

In our discussion of the dream, I suggested the policemen represented her lively relationship with the law – she was always judging herself and others, putting them on trial, as it were – and that the result of this relationship was a dead world. This interpretation didn't produce a click, mainly because it cast something that was experienced positively in the dream as something negative. It thus wasn't true to the experience of the dream.

Here, the evidence of the dream – the experience of it – didn't support an interpretation, and lends validity to Isabelle's lack of a click in response.

6

Working with
Your Dreams

Getting Started with Dream Work

I've been working with dreams for over 30 years, but that doesn't mean that when I have or hear a dream its meaning is clear to me. Quite the contrary: most often, I haven't a clue what it means. I may be able to make a few links with what has happened during the previous day, or with dreams I've recently remembered (or in the case with a dream group, heard), but this in itself isn't enough to give me any real understanding of the dream.

Of course, there is the odd dream the meaning of which hits you like a thunderbolt as soon as you remember it. And this experience is much more common when you have asked for a Solution Dream (see pages 32–41), the night before. As I emphasized in the chapter on Solution Dreams, you have a huge advantage if you know what question the dream is striving to answer. But, for the most part, you really do have to work with dreams to understand what they are saying. Perhaps I can best explain why with an example.

Ben's Dream
Just before Christmas, Ben, aged four and a half, had a dream in which his mother came down the chimney bringing presents for Christmas. He told her the dream in the morning. His mother (who had recently done one of my dream workshops) thought the dream meant Ben was ready to know the truth. She gently suggested that perhaps his mummy was Santa Claus? Ben laughed at this preposterous idea and gave it not another moment's thought.

Ben's dream is completely straightforward to us. There is no attempt to conceal its meaning *in the dream*. For Ben, however, it goes against something which he knows is true – Santa Claus is real and brings presents down the chimney. The dream, therefore, must be the aberration.

Where is the problem here? It lies in Ben's inability to recognize the truth of the dream, because it comes up against something he knows and is very attached to – the existence of Santa Claus.

The Obvious
Like with Ben, the meaning of a dream often runs against something we are attached to – an image of ourselves or of others. If we have a dream of lusting after our brother's wife, or wishing to steal money from the bank where we work, we gloss over it because such thoughts (and actions) are immoral. They are not how we wish to think of ourselves.

These are examples of the way in which the unconscious is right under our nose, not hidden

Often, you're unaware of something because you're just too close to it and don't want to see it. The unconscious in these cases is the obvious.

away somewhere in "the unconscious mind". Often, you're unaware of something because you're just too close to it and don't want to see it. The unconscious in these cases is the obvious.

Getting Distance

When the difficulty is that you can't see the wood for the trees, the solution is to get some distance. This is particularly the case when you're working with your own dreams. (When you hear the dreams of others, or work with your own dreams in a group or one-to-one, there is already a distance by virtue of the others present.)

There are two basic ways to get distance when you're working with your own dreams. Putting time between you and your dream and putting your dream into language.

Time

Putting time between you and your dream is straightforward: record your dream in your dream diary, with its accompanying associations, day residue, and what is going on in your life. Put your dream book aside. Then look back over your dreams from the distance of a month, or several months. Meanings that were previously hidden from you become transparent.

The disadvantage of this technique is obvious. Any timely warnings or information that your dream had for you will be missed. You'll have the benefit of hindsight, but not of the ongoing daily dialogue. For this reason, using time to get distance is best used with dreams you can't crack at the time – look back at these dreams, and your work with them, from the distance of several months and often everything will be clear.

Language

Working with your dreams in the day or so after you dream them is your best way forward. In part, such work is aimed at putting what is obvious to you (your unconscious assumptions) into words, so that they become visible. You do this by fleshing out the dream imagery with the associations and thoughts

that went into creating it. This work also aims at giving you the distance to see yourself more like others see you and at helping you accept emotions, feelings, points of view and thoughts that feel wrong to entertain.

In the next sections I'll outline a number of basic techniques for putting your dreams into words, and creating the distance you need to be able to reflect on them.

Getting to Know the Basic Techniques

I've tried to make my descriptions of the basic techniques clear, and to keep any intimidating examples to a minimum. What matters is not what I and others have learned from their dreams – but what *you* learn.

And the only way you will learn is through experience. It's by doing the exercises that you'll get a feel for when each technique is appropriate, for example, which dream images should be associated to, or explored by, the "What is" or "I am" techniques, or when Clarifying the Dream should be used to get the big picture.

Getting Started

Probably the best way to begin is to read one of the technique sections the night before you have a dream, and then apply it the following morning when you wake up. Don't aim to try to understand your dream completely. Instead, try to get a sense of the power of the technique. You will probably need to work with several dreams before you feel confident that you are applying the technique correctly and getting a sense of what it can reveal. Aim to spend at least 15 minutes working with each technique on a dream. Even working with one technique at a time should enable your dreams to begin to speak to you.

Once you have mastered one technique, move on to the next, and so on, until you finish using the basic five. With Dream Language, it might be best to look over the dreams you've already recorded and worked with rather than to work with a new one.

This is because getting a sense of the play of language in your dream and dream account is best done when the concrete reality of the experience has somewhat faded, and you can look at your language itself rather than what it describes. This is especially true when working on your own.

Working with Dreams

Once you've got a sense of what each technique can contribute to understanding your dreams, you'll want to start to use the techniques in combination.

Initially, use Clarifying the Dream to get the big picture, and then one of the techniques that helps reveal the meaning of the individual dream images. Don't be too ambitious. At the beginning, understanding everything in the dream is not a realistic aim – Freud, who was no novice when it came to dream interpretation, thought it impossible. There are many levels of meaning and understanding. Even a single one should increase your appreciation of the wisdom and creativity of your dreams.

Expand Your Repertoire

Everyone has favourite dream-work techniques. They may be taken from the basic five, or from the examples I've given when talking about individual dream theorists. These techniques will be the ones that ring a bell for you.

This is a natural tendency, but do try to subvert it occasionally. Look over the book and find a technique you haven't used recently – for example, looking for the objective versus subjective meaning of dream images, Hillman's technique of capitalizing dream characters and actions, or amplification – and apply it to the next dream you have. Try to do this at least once every two weeks. Over time, it will enhance your dream work as it expands your repertoire of techniques.

Clarifying the Dream

This technique consists of a series of questions about your dream. Answering them will give you the "big picture" – a broad perspective of your dream and its meaning. As the aim here is to give you some distance from the immediacy of having dreamed, ideally you record your answers in a written form. Both in writing your responses and in reading them over, you'll find that aspects of the dream's meaning will leap into consciousness. Particularly in the beginning, it's worth reading over your written responses after a period of time, say 24 hours. This will enable you to take advantage of both distancing mechanisms – time and putting the dream into language.

Dream Locations

What are the scene(s) of action in the dream? What possibilities do they present you with?

Every dream is composed of one or more scenes. Think of them as locations for a movie. In a movie, each location is chosen to highlight a particular set of possibilities. For example, a desert often gives the hero an extreme and usually beautiful environment that will test his capacity to survive. In a movie, each location is there to show what the hero is made of. Is he at home in an city, on a beach, in a school playground, with a beautiful man/woman?

Each location in a dream similarly presents particular challenges and a particular psychological, personal, and sometimes bodily, space. You can do different things in a kitchen than in a study. Similarly, a dense dark forest makes you feel, think, and act differently than an open sunny field. For example, Peter recently had a dream in which:

I found two plastic containers on my bed. They were open and you could smell the decomposed bodies of two people. I needed help to get rid of them and asked someone to help me.

We soon realized the decomposed bodies were those of his parents. We had been talking about the way he hadn't been able to mourn their deaths properly and that, as a result, they were around him like a bad smell. But I wondered why they were sitting on his bed, in the bedroom. It emerged his unmourned parents were affecting both his ability to sleep and his love life.

If your dream is situated in a house or other kind of building, note where the scene of the action is. If there is a message about your body in the dream, it will often be signalled by this location – an attic can signify your head; the toilet, your ability to eliminate; and so on.

The dream environment can show you how you see the world, especially when it is similar from night to night. A good way of starting to orient yourself in relation to the dream is to describe each dream locality and become aware of the possibilities it presents you with.

People in the Dream

Who are the main dream characters?

Who are the figures who populate the dream? Are they people you know? Are they from a particular period on your life? (Here we are doing a simple listing of the dream characters. To flesh out their meanings, use the three Working with Dream Elements techniques, see pages 93–101.)

Choices

Answer either a) or b).

a) What is my path in the dream? How did I make choices?

In answering this question, you're trying to

Clarifying the Dream

Write down the answers to the following questions:

1   What are the scene(s) of action in the dream?

2   Who are the main dream characters?

3   What is my path in the dream? Think of yourself as a film hero(ine) – what are the choices you make and how do you make them?
or
How do you make choices? Are you able to move beyond the pressing dream possibilities? Consider this by listing the choices you make in the dream and on a 1–5 scale rate how much they are shaped by your perception of the dream environment.

4   What are the issues in the dream? The conflicts? The unresolved situations?

5   Is there any word play in the dream?

6   What is my mood in the dream overall? In the individual scenes? What possibilities does this attunement give me? How does this accord with my waking life?

7   What images, relationships and resolutions in the dream feel positive?

8   What images, relationships and resolutions feel negative?

9   What is the dream responding to in my life?

10   What connections does this dream have with other dreams I've had?

illuminate your action (and lack of action) in the dream. Again, use the example of a film. A heroine is defined by the choices she makes – for example, does she approach her adversary and invite conflict, does she try to talk and resolve things, or does she run away?

What are the defining choices in this dream? What kind of a hero(ine) are you? Rewrite the dream emphasizing each choice and how you make it. For example, some choices you make because you are following other people, some because you want to, some because they seem right or fair, some to please others, some because they seem the easiest path, some because you feel perverse or contrary, etc.

b) When you make your dream choices, are you able to move beyond the pressing dream possibilities? Consider this by listing the choices you make in the dream and, on a 1–5 scale, rating how much they are shaped by your perception of the dream environment.

Most of our choices are determined by how we see the world. If we are confronted with a dangerous snake in a dream, we run, or wake up. But even when faced with such a snake, we can have many different interactions. If we have some distance, we might choose to engage it in conversation, enlist it in aiding us, or frighten it by making elephant noises.

Now that you are awake, look at your dream choices again and see if you can think of different ways of responding to the same situation. Think of what determined your dream response.

Issues, Conflicts, Situations

What are the issues in the dream? The conflicts? The unresolved situations?

By issues we mean anything in the dream that raises a question for you; they do not have to be matters of life and death. Conflicts would include both internal conflicts – where you are in two minds about some decision or action – and external conflicts, with other dream characters. Unresolved situations would include situations that are literally unresolved (the

SAMPLE EXERCISE

Dream: It was dark and icy and I was on a plane. My brother and his wife were waiting on the runway in the back seat of a black car. I was in the plane and I had to give my brother a book. It had a treasure map on the back. He was supposed to give me another book in return. The plane was just about to take off. I ran down the back stairs to his car and gave it to him quickly. Then I ran toward the plane to get back on … I shouted to him to come quickly and give me my book. They were closing the back door of the plane. He came and gave me a jar of Nutella instead, handing it to me with very long pincers (like the ones used for a barbecue). I grabbed the jar and jumped onto the plane and just made it to my chair in time before the plane took off …

What is the scene of action?
An anonymous airport at night. It was cold and dark.

Who are the main dream characters?
My brother Alfredo and myself.

What is my path in the dream?
I chose to get off the plane to give my brother the treasure map even though I feared the plane would take off without me. I ran to him and then back, waiting near the plane for him to give me something in return. I shouted at him to hurry. I took the Nutella and jumped back on the plane. I felt disappointed with the Nutella -- I wanted a book for the flight.

What are the defining choices in this dream?
Will I risk getting off the plane to give my brother the book? I felt I had to. I'd given my word.

What are the issues in the dream? The conflicts? The unresolved situations?
The big issue and unresolved situation is that I gave my brother what he needed in the present, but he gave me something I'd liked as a child. I felt let down that he

didn't give me a book as I had nothing to read on the plane …

Is there any word play in the dream?
Nutella seems a word play on "nuts." In Italian, a nut, "la noce," is female.

What images, relationships and resolutions in the dream feel positive?
I was able to give my brother the book and I insisted on him giving me something back. I made it back to my seat before the plane took off (just about!)

What images, relationships and resolutions feel negative?
I was rushing like a lunatic to get things done. I didn't receive my full reward in the end or at least what I was expecting to receive. I was disappointed and thought I deserved more …

What is the dream responding to in my life?
I suppose looking at the question above, I'm always going well out of my way to help people and I never really get much back in return. With my family, I feel resentful that I'm always making the effort to see them. This is a weight on my shoulders.

What connections does this dream have with other dreams I've had?
I have had many dreams about planes recently and also about books as gifts. I don't know yet what they mean.

Summary: This exercise highlighted the fact that I rush around trying to help people and don't pay much attention to what the real issues are in my life. The jar of Nutella I get in return seems to imply I'm "nuts" to put myself out in this way, and that it doesn't get me what I want. Perhaps it also indicates my family see and treat me as a little girl, and don't really see who I am and what I need in the present.

dream ends or fades before you find out) and those in which you feel dissatisfied with the way they're resolved (in the dream, and afterwards).

In terms of Jung's description of dreams as drama (see box on page 60) we're trying to articulate what trees you find yourself stuck in, or halfway up (regardless of whether you get down).

List the issues, conflicts and unresolved situations in the dream.

Word Play

Is there any word play in the dream? (See Dream Language, page 89.)

Mood

What is my mood in the dream overall? In the individual scenes? What possibilities does this attunement give me? How does this accord with my waking life?

Our mood is our attunement to the world. When we feel excited, the world shows us infinite possibilities; when we feel low, events bring us down.

Positive Elements

What images, relationships and resolutions in the dream feel healing or positive?

Negative Elements

What images, relationships and resolutions feel negative?

Connections to My Life

What is the dream responding to in my life?
In listing the links to your day world, do you have a clearer sense of this? Or is it more that you connect different scenes in the dream with different live events?

Connections with Other Dreams

What connections does this dream have with other dreams I've had?
Thinking about recent dreams, do the symbols, events, and/or moods ring bells for you?

Mapping Your Dreams

Use the chart below to map your dreams over a period of time. List the date of the dream and *no more than three* of the following: the strongest feelings/moods in the dream, the main dream characters (apart from yourself), the most powerful imagery and dream actions, and the main dream locations. This will give you a way to catch common dream elements, which you can then explore using the techniques that follow.

Date of dream	Strong feelings in dream	Dream characters Male Female	Dream imagery Positive Negative	Dream actions Yours Others	Dream locations

Dream Language

Our access to dreams is largely through language. The way you put your dreams into words – for yourself and others – isn't random. It's part and parcel of the dream's message. The difficulty in hearing this message, as in so much dream work, is getting some distance from it. By dream language I mean both the language and word play in the dream – as in the names of places, objects and people, and the language we use when communicating and recording our dreams while under the influence of the dream itself.

Dreams and Poetry

Many writers on dreams have come to the conclusion that the closest approximation to dream language in waking life is poetry. Poetic imagery is elliptical, condensed and has many levels of meaning. It utilizes images rather than facts and prefers particular images to general ones. It doesn't use conjunctions and aims to communicate through the experience the poem conveys.

In all this, poetry is essentially similar to the language of dreams but it lacks one element –– dreams use humour in their word play much more often than poetry. Dreams delight in using puns, plays on words and word opposites. Such humour is part of the way dreams convey meanings. Slips of the tongue when telling a dream, and of the pen when writing it, are all part of the dream's armory in conveying experience and meaning.

Respect for Language

This section is aimed at helping you become more aware of the poetry and humour in your dream language. The first step is a respect for language itself.

Studies show that children's dreams become more like those of adults – complicated, elliptical and condensed – as their capacity to use language develops. The sea of language we live in during the day is the same sea we swim in at night. Dreams are not opposed to language – they are language at play in us at night.

Of course, as we awake, we're aware that often it's difficult to put our dreams into words and that as we do this something can be lost. It is the same difficulty that novelists and writers have – that of conveying the rich texture of life in appropriate language. In writing down our dreams, we all become novelists of the night.

As I've noted earlier, the first thing you should write down are unusual names – of people and places. These easily fade and become muddled if you don't record them immediately. These names often contain the most poetic of our language play – condensation, ellipsis, and word plays of all sorts.

But also be aware of the way you write your dream down. If you put down one word when you mean to write another, don't erase it. Instead, score through the word lightly and write the word you meant to write next to it. Such mistakes are slips of the pen. Freud has taught us that such slips are not purely mistakes, but aim to convey another level of the dream's meaning. Both the word you wrote and the word you meant to write are important in the dream's interpretation. (The same is true of slips when telling the dream – the word or name you didn't mean to say is just as important as the word you did.)

Perhaps the best way to help you become aware of the word play in dreams is a refresher course in poetic language. An appreciation of this will heighten your awareness of similar language in your dreams.

Figurative Language

Literal language means exactly what it says. The language of poetry and dreams is figurative. It changes the literal meaning to express different meanings, to refresh or expand the meaning of the original, or to convey complexity.

The simplest of the poetic figures of speech is the simile. A simile links two different things by the use of words such as "like", or "as". For example, "My love is like a red, red rose" and "I wandered lonely as a cloud". But similes are not limited to "poetic language". We use them all the time. "My boss is like a bull when he gets mad", or "My friend dresses like a movie star".

A simile without "like" or "as" is a metaphor. "The neck of the woods", or the "foot of the mountain" are common ones, as is the equation of team or company with a family – "we're not a company, we're one big happy family".

Personification is giving otherwise abstract or inanimate objects human characteristics – for example, "the skies wept" "the tree glowered" or "the wind whispered". Emily Dickinson's "The Railway Train", is a poetic example:

I like to see it lap up the miles,
And lick the valleys up,
And stop to feed itself at tanks;
And then, prodigious, step ...

Our dream environment is often alive with personification. The following example from Sam includes both personification and word play:

I was selling my company. I dreamt that I was filling my car with diesel instead of premium petrol. I couldn't figure it out.

Sam was in the process of selling a company he'd built up from scratch. The dream made his wife wonder if he was as comfortable as he thought about doing this. He expected the money he was to make from the sale was going to make his car/life (personification) run for a long time. In the dream,

he puts *die sel(l)* in the car. It shows that he fears losing the company will be like a death.

Another frequent dream visitor is hyperbole. Dreams often use exaggeration to make their point. Humour is often an accompaniment. Ordinary language is full of hyperbole. Well-worn examples include, "a flood of tears", "tons of money", "waiting for ages".

Word for Word

Perhaps the most common form of word play in a dream is that in which the dream uses an image – jeans for example, to refer to a similar sounding word – genes. A common example – a dream in which you are pestered by insects – can indicate you are being "bugged" by something.

Jean asked for a Solution Dream about a coffee house she owned, which was losing money. In the dream that followed, she was thinking about the coffee house as she sat near a swimming pool. Suddenly, a wild boar appeared and gored her. We arrived at the interpretation that she was "bored" with the drama of the failing coffee shop, and also with the way it was draining away her blood (energy, money).

In another example, the play on words is enacted in the dream …

I dreamed that someone was following me and he was going to "shoot" me. I imagined it was a sub-machine gun but it turned out to be an old fashioned tripod camera and he wanted to shoot my photo!

Tips for Catching Your Dream Word Play

1 **Read your dreams aloud**
Word play can involve words that sound alike (jeans/genes, boar/bore), or read differently than they sound (diesel/die sell). Reading your dreams aloud can help you catch both.

2 **Reading your dreams**
Can also help you catch dream expressions such as left holding the baby, falling between two stools.

3 **Look at any unusual words closely**
Do they break up into two words? Does one part of the word sound different from the way it looks? How is it pronounced?

4 **Imagine your dream as a cartoon**
What expression would be used to précis it? This technique enabled John to realize he was being led up the garden path.

5 **Word play**
Some people have a real talent for catching word play in dreams. I'm not one, but working at it has helped me greatly improve.

Dreams can also have word/images that break down into two or more words, as in the example on page 90 of die-sel.

Isabelle, a member of a dream group, had the following dream:

I was with my mother. We were watching television. There were several very fat women on the television. I said to my mother, "they're amorphous, like you." She disagreed vociferously with me, saying, "I'm not amorphous."

When she woke up, Isabelle was very pleased her mother had disagreed with her. Her mother (and subsequently she) had always found it difficult to disagree with or be separate from another. In this dream she puts her mother down, but her mother stands up for herself, something she rarely did in the day world.

On one level, the dream indicates Isabelle is starting to separate from her mother. The dream also has an interesting play on words. Amorphous can be broken down into "amour" and "fuss", fuss about "amour" or love. For Isabelle, one of the legacies of her decidedly difficult relationship with her parents was that in every relationship (however social or casual) her main concern was whether or not she

was loved. The dream indicates that less fuss about amour would be a step toward the separation from her parents and others she craves.

Dream Expressions

Many metaphorical expressions in our language can be literally embodied in dreams. Such expressions as "fallen woman", "going down the drain", "left holding the baby", "pulling one's socks up", "sitting on the fence" and "changing one's tune", can all literally occur in dreams.

John had a dream in which he was working in his garden when an attractive girl appeared at the fence at the bottom of the garden.

She called me over seductively. Intrigued, I went over to meet her, but when I got there, she had disappeared.

The dream caused him to realize he was being "led up the garden path" by a woman he had been dating.

Associations

While you're dreaming, your brain is flooded with chemicals that maximize your ability to make connections – connections with your past, with facts you have learned, your perceptions and deductions, and with all aspects of your present life. Freud had intuited something similar, when he speculated that our dream images are a result of an unconscious process of association, in which the images with the most potent, relevant and numerous associations are those that are chosen to be in our dreams.

Making associations to dream images is one of the most powerful ways of finding out why this particular image is in the dream. It enables us to understand the unique specificity of dream images. Dream images are never chosen randomly, and are never generic – we never dream of a house, but only of a very particular house, with specific qualities.

There are two main kinds of associations in relation to dreams: short-chain associations and long-chain associations. The first are associated with Jung's dream work, the second with Freud's.

Short-Chain Associations

These are simply the first thoughts that occur to us in relation to a dream image. For example, I recently had a dream in which I was in the basement of the house where I grew up. Part of the dream involved me having to turn out the lights, and being scared of what might happen. As I arrived at the stairs to the ground floor, I saw a little man with a blue face ahead of me. On waking, I wondered why the little man had a blue face.

My first association to the little man was to a robot able to walk up stairs I'd seen on television with my daughter. I then realized the television show was called *Blue Peter*. In this short-chain association, my first association to the dream clarifies one meaning of the little man's face – colour.

It is important to recognize that you can have several short- and long-chain associations to each dream image, giving you different layers of meaning. It is important to follow up each chain of

Dream images are never chosen randomly, and are never generic.

associations and not be satisfied with the first, especially as in my *Blue Peter* example. Here an association gives me a meaning of the little man and colour blue, but it is not an especially telling one, in that it didn't answer the question of why this little man was put in my childhood basement.

Long-Chain Associations

These involve following the train of signifiers beyond the first and obvious association. The robot on *Blue Peter* was called Asimo – a clear reference, I explained to my daughter, to Isaac Asimov, a science fiction writer who wrote the *Three Laws of Robotics*. As she wasn't the slightest bit interested in this, I mused on silently, remembering when I used to read a lot of science fiction, when sick as a child.

This long chain of associations led me back to my childhood, to the time when I lived in the house with the scary basement, and it reminded me of how very ill I'd been. In fact, at the time I had this dream the asthma that had afflicted me in childhood was very little in evidence. It was as if the dream was reminding me of this, and perhaps of how little I appreciate the way my life has changed.

What Should You Associate To?

Freud asked his patients to associate to every single element of the dream. But even the most diligent analysts tend to focus on a limited number of dream images and elements.

Remember, when I talk about dream images I am not just talking about dream characters but also elements of the environment. Why this basement? Why this staircase? You always need to try to understand the meaning of this specific element in this specific dream.

How Do You Associate?

Associations are not produced by the rational mind. (Remember the chemicals associated with rational thinking are reduced to zero during REM sleep.) So there is no point in trying to "figure them out".

Rather, let go of reason's grasp and get into a state of reverie. Wonder about the dream and feel its magic and mystery. Let yourself feel the image in your mind. Let your mind freewheel. Let thoughts pop into your head and be curious about the other thoughts that might connect to them. Don't worry about whether these associations make sense. That will come later. When you have the chain of associations, write them down. Then go back to the same dream image and repeat the process, until nothing else comes.

What Now?

You'll have written down different thoughts and images that your dream elements have evoked. Still in a half-state of reverie, look at them and see if you can find elements in common, associations to similar times in your life – to similar events or simply associations that really speak to you – that are evocative of the meaning of the dream image.

Add these meanings to any sense you have already made of the dream – use associations to *flesh out* the meaning of the dream images, not to replace them.

WHICH DREAM ELEMENTS SHOULD YOU FOCUS ON?

Choose the images that are
- Puzzling
- Unusual
- Powerful
- Composite – the image seems thrown together from two different sources

What Is ...

What Is is a powerful technique derived from the work of Medard Boss and Martin Heidegger. Their war cry was, "There is nothing behind the phenomena. The truth is in the phenomena themselves."

In other words everything we need to know is already *in* the dream images but we don't (yet) see it.

What Is aims at explicating individual elements of a dream. To do this, you simply describe in detail the settings, characters and feelings of your dream. The power of this technique is that it puts your unconscious assumptions into words.

For example, if you dream of a cat, there are all sorts of interpretations that can be made – a cat represents the feminine, selfishness, narcissism, etc. Such interpretations may have their truths, but they are not specific to *your* dream cat.

To find out more about your particular dream cat, describe it in great detail. This is a description from Bill of a cat in his dream:

He was a bit bedraggled, a bit the worse for wear. His ear was missing a good chunk – it looked like he'd lost it in a fight. His grey fur wasn't in good shape. But he had an air about him. He was proud and undaunted. I could see this would get him into trouble at times, but it also made him someone you'd like on your side.

None of this would have come out in a generic interpretation of a dream cat. As he described this war-torn animal, Bill realized that his dream cat reminded him of a friend who'd just gone through a difficult divorce and was much the worse for wear. Bill had been rather critical of his friend for being so down at the mouth, but he realized the dream was showing him that his friend still had a lot to offer.

In making a link to his friend, Bill was making a link to his day world. You should try to do this with each dream description you do.

everything we need to know is already in the dream images but we don't (yet) see it.

Who Is ...

You can use the same technique to describe people you know and celebrities or strangers. Assume you're talking to someone from an entirely different culture, who doesn't have any of the same cultural references. This makes it necessary for you to put all the things you know into words.

For example, a client in individual therapy told a dream in which Tony Soprano, the eponymous character from the hit TV series, appeared. I asked, "Who is Tony Soprano?" He said, "You know who he is!" I replied, "Pretend I don't …" He went on to give this description.

He's a mafia boss. A big guy with big appetites. He always has a couple of women on the go. He kills people as easily as you'd flush a toilet. You'd never know to look at him… it looks like he's got it made – money, power, women, everything… but the thing is, he's struggling within himself. He's seeing this shrink and he's… trying to work something out. You can see he's great at what he does, but he doesn't want to be doing it.

Everyone has a different Tony Soprano. Some people would be revolted by his violence and the way he betrays his wife. My client admires him. "His Tony Soprano" has it made, can express all his aggression freely, and can satisfy all his appetites. But there is a worm in the apple. In spite of this, he's not happy. My client was a "big beast" in the financial industry, able to indulge his aggression and appetites. But, much to his own surprise, he had come to see me "to work something out". Through this work, he discovered that though he was extremely successful – "great at what he does" – he wasn't really enjoying his work.

In discovering the parallels between Tony Soprano and himself, my client was making the link between his dream and the day world. Importantly, this link showed him something new about himself: it legitimized his desire to "work something out" by making a parallel with one of his heroes.

Settings

Where does your dream take place? Even the most anonymous setting can be described and reveal untold riches. Famous places, too, need to be described, as your Louvre Museum is different from mine. Describe your dream settings as if you are speaking to a listener who hasn't a clue about what you're talking about.

In a recent dream group, a dreamer found herself lost in Harrow. I asked what was Harrow?

Harrow is a town outside London. I dread going there. It's neither fish nor fowl, neither city nor country. It's suburban. I would have ended up in the suburbs, but I made a decision to go a different way. It was the right decision for me. I have a friend who lives there – but my relationship with her isn't going anywhere.

It emerged that, having uprooted herself from her native country to take an immensely satisfying job, the dreamer felt herself to be betwixt and between socially. She feared the ties of relationship, but was tired of being alone. She was living in "Harrow". Of course, the town's name also involves a play on words – harrow, harrowing. This adds another level to its meaning.

This town, neither fish nor fowl, enabled the dreamer to make a link with her harrowing day world social situation, and made her feel the urgency of changing it.

Don't be afraid to apply the What Is technique to the humblest of settings – a corner shop, a bicycle rack, a front garden. You'll find there's no such thing as a mundane dream setting once you've started to unpack its meaning.

Feelings

Finally, apply the What Is technique to the feelings in the dream. Of course, if we all don't know what sadness is in general, there would be no point in telling anyone you're sad. But like "your Tony Soprano", your "sadness" is different from mine.

Using the What Is technique with feelings involves using evocative imagery to describe your feelings. Recently a client said she felt adrift, but not like a small boat in the English Channel that was about to be run down. It was helpful to know what being adrift was not for her, but she was unable to say what kind of boat she was in, and what kind of sea. Becoming aware of this lack of clarity can provoke further thoughts or dreams.

The Entire What Is Process

1 **List the key elements in your dream**
If you've done a breakdown using the Clarifying the Dream technique you can use that list of settings, characters and feelings. If not, make a list for the purposes of this technique.

2 **Describe the key elements**
The ideal is to describe every element of the dream, but if you, like most of us, have limited time, describe those images or dream elements that stand out, which just don't make sense, or are unusual.

    If you are working by yourself, write your descriptions down or speak into a voice recorder. Remember, your dreaming mind has chosen this particular person, place, or feeling for a reason – or more likely, many reasons. To find out these reasons, you have to bring what is "inside" the dream image out. Making a record of this process is part of what enables you to externalize and thus see what is in the image.

    Remember to aim at a description that is so complete someone who didn't know you or your world would understand it. Don't stint on individual descriptions, rather do fewer. (You may find the whole process so fascinating you end up doing more than you intended!)

3 **The third step is to make a link to your day world**
In all the examples cited in the last few pages, the dreamer was able to make a link as soon as they heard themselves describe their dream character or setting. But sometimes this step is a bit more difficult – if what you are describing is tucked a bit too tightly under your nose, so to speak.

    Try asking yourself a few questions. In the Harrow example on page 96 you'd ask "what in my life do I dread that is neither fish nor fowl?" In the cat example on page 95, you'd ask "who do I know that's like a bedraggled, beaten up grey cat, but still proud and undaunted?"

    Making a link or connection to the day world is the third step of the "What Is" process. After making the link between your day world and your dream descriptions, you should have a good sense of why this particular image has appeared in your dream.

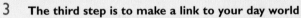

I Am ...

I Am is a technique from Gestalt therapy, and it's based on the assumption that everything in the dream represents a part of yourself, projected outwards.

Cheryl had the following dream:

A man is driving a sports car down a twisty mountain road. I'm going just that bit too fast and feel slightly out of control. I stamp on the brakes, but they don't respond and I wake in a panic.

This is the sort of dream to which it's easy to attach a general meaning – we'd guess there's an area in Cheryl's life in which she was going too fast; she was out of control. (Although we'd wonder why a man was driving ...) But we've learned to be suspicious of dreams that seem to yield fruit so easily. We're aware that there are other levels of meaning which we are ignoring.

To use I Am – you imagine you are the car and you feel your way into its character and possibilities, talking aloud as you do so. You'll have to overcome your self-consciousness to do this. You'll also have to get beyond your first couple of statements, which probably won't tell you more than you already know. "I'm a sports car. I go very fast." Just let yourself embody the car and keep talking, trying to articulate what you know about yourself as the image in the dream. You'll be surprised what comes out.

Cheryl started in the usual way:

I'm a sports car. I go very fast.

But then, her monologue began to veer away from the expected:

It's what I'm made for. Men are attracted to me. I'm made to attract them and to tempt them to go too fast. They do it, and then get into trouble. They crash. It makes me happy and I laugh.

I asked "But when they crash, don't you get damaged?" She replied, "I never considered that." She imagined what would happen when her dream car went out of control and crashed. It was a sobering experience.

Up until this point, Cheryl had regarded herself as the victim of a foolish marriage in which her husband had gone bankrupt after running up huge debts. Her victim status had been enhanced when she had first attempted to address the problem in counselling. Her inexperienced male counsellor had been drawn into an inappropriate involvement with her. She had then dumped him as a weak man.

I'd been aware of her seductive manner, but until this dream had not been able to get her to see her involvement in this, and in the previous disasters which "befell" her. The I Am technique brought this alive for her.

Involvement

The I Am technique is often useful in enabling you to connect with your emotional involvement in what happens to you and why, to move beyond an intellectual understanding of the dream.

Cheryl then used the I Am technique to embody the twisty mountain road and the brakes. In each case, she learned something about how she had come to take up this way of interacting with men. The twisty mountain road, when embodied, made her realize how twisted her exciting and dangerous relationship with her father was. The lack of brakes helped her connect to the way her mother had been unable to put the brakes on their inappropriate relationship.

Unusual Images

This technique is especially useful for images which don't make sense to you. Alan was an extremely intellectual middle-aged professor with a pronounced beer belly. I normally wouldn't comment on this, but his stomach was an active participant in the sessions, growling, rumbling, gurgling and occasionally even producing a noise that sounded like a mouse squeaking. The sounds were so noticeable that sometimes I felt as if there were three of us in the room. However, Alan was seemingly oblivious to his stomach's contributions to our meetings.

One day, after I'd unsuccessfully drawn his attention to a particularly noticeable growl – "Sorry if it bothers you, I'm probably just hungry" – he reported a vivid dream fragment.

A hairy stomach is chasing me around the room. It has very sharp teeth and I'm trying to get away.

After telling the dream, he said, "It's strange, but though I was running away, I didn't think the stomach meant me harm."

Attempts to have Alan associate to the stomach met a defensive reaction – "It's a disgusting fat hairy stomach, what else do you need to know?" I then asked him to become the stomach. After a halting start, "I'm a stomach. I'm too big," and a long silence, the words suddenly poured out:

I'm angry. No, I'm furious. What do I have to do to get your attention? ... You ignore me and run away from me! Don't you know I'm here? It's as though you don't know you have a body ... I've been storing your feelings for years. Your anger, your hatred, your love, your desire. Just so you can swan around and make objective pronouncements! I'm fed up. If you don't start listening to me I'm going to make serious trouble ... Is that what you want? Because I'm ready for a fight. I don't want to be left holding the baby any more.

I had never seen Alan so alive. (Interestingly, his stomach made not a peep during this monologue.) After it, there was a long silence. "I've been trying to avoid this moment," he said to me. "I'm afraid of my stomach. It's ridiculous, isn't it?" After a long pause, I said, "You're afraid of feeling." He started to cry.

This moment was a breakthrough in his therapy. Whenever he was too much in his "head" after this, I'd say, "what does your stomach have to say?" and he'd be able to connect to his feelings.

Dialogues

When you feel more at home with the I Am technique, you can initiate dialogue between yourself and the dream elements – between you and the road, for example, or between you and the (absent) brakes. In Gestalt therapy proper, you'd put one of the participants in the dialogue (the road, the brakes) into a nearby chair and have a dialogue with it. Again, recording this dialogue and listening to it later is a good way to get some distance when working on your own.

Moving on Recurrent Dreams

Try the following with your recurrent dreams, to see if you can move them on:

1   **Pay particular attention to the details of your recurrent dreams**
    You'll find that some elements stay more or less the same, but others change over time. Try to define what it is that stays the same. Then notice how even that which stays the same changes in subtle ways.

2   **Use the What Is technique**
    To describe the "stuckness" in as much detail as you can.

3   **Associate to it**
    To get a picture of the connections it makes with other aspects of your life. Don't be too easily satisfied here. A recurrent dream is trying to tell you something new about something old. Don't just stop after one significant association – especially if it tells you something you already know. For example;
    Recurrent dream: I'm having to give a presentation in front of my French teacher.
    Unenlightening association: I'm nervous about giving a talk to colleagues on Friday.

4   **Use the I Am technique**
    To have the situation speak. Our aim here is not simply just to understand the dream better, but to enable the stuckness in you to have its say. Think about the stuckness as being similar to Alan's stomach (see page 99). It has something to say to you. Let it speak.

5   **Many recurrent dreams have an element of lucidity to them – you're aware at some point that this is all happening again**
    Often during such dreams, you use your dawning lucidity to wake yourself up. Look at the following section "Nightmares" and at the chapter on lucid dreaming (see pages 130–41) to become more aware during the dream and to change the old dream pattern.

Recurrent Dreams

In dreams, as in life, we can find ourselves seemingly stuck in situations that happen again and again. In life, it may be a similar pattern of relationship with a partner, a boss or a child. In dreams, recurrent situations can span a much wider range of situations. Common ones are returning to school or college, being about to take an exam – and being totally unprepared, or finding yourself naked, or nearly so, in public.

Being stuck in this way is always a sign that something is unprocessed, and your dreams are attempting to help you move beyond this block. It is this moving beyond, rather than simply understanding, which is the aim of such dreams. Often, without having any particular understanding of the dream, you find they gradually change, become rarer, and then stop.

John had recurrent dreams of his mouth being stuck together with a gummy substance. He would then attempt to remove it, pulling out seemingly never-ending strings of the stuff. In the course of our work, we explored his sticky relationship with his mother and others who he always wanted to please. As he moved on from these relationships, in which, so to speak, everyone was a version of his mother, the dream started to change. The gummy stuff

Understanding can be a way of moving recurrent dreams on, but isn't essential. In life, as in dreams, we often change without particularly knowing why.

became less gummy, then there was less and less of it. In the end, the stuff disappeared, and he stopped dreaming of his mouth. This happened without us really understanding what the gummy stuff in his mouth "really" was or very much about this odd dream symptom at all.

Understanding can be a way of moving recurrent dreams on, but isn't essential. In life, as in dreams, we often change without particularly knowing why.

Nightmares

When many people think of dreams, they think of nightmares – those fear-inducing, disturbing dreams that wake us from the deepest sleep, shading the first hours of our day. Statistically, we have no more nightmares than pleasant dreams. But for those who remember dreams rarely, nightmares are often the only dreams they recall, the only dreams that break through their repression of dreams.

Simply remembering more dreams will change this, as it will inevitably lead to remembering more positive dreams. The techniques in this chapter can help further by enabling you to change your nightmares into dreams where you conquer your fears.

Child's Play

My six-year-old daughter had been waking up night after night with dreams about vampires. I'd tried to tell her we could stop them, to no avail. Daddies don't know how to fight vampires.

One night I told her a story about Boobela the girl giant, a character I'd made up. Boobela was suffering from nightmares about vampires. Now she was frightened to go to sleep. My daughter sat up in bed.

Boobela had decided to visit the Dream People because she'd heard they knew a lot about dreams and nightmares. The head of the Dream People told Boobela how, when he was her age, he had nightmares about vampires, but that he had learned to stop them. Was Boobela interested in this? YES! He told her he had learned to call his friends into

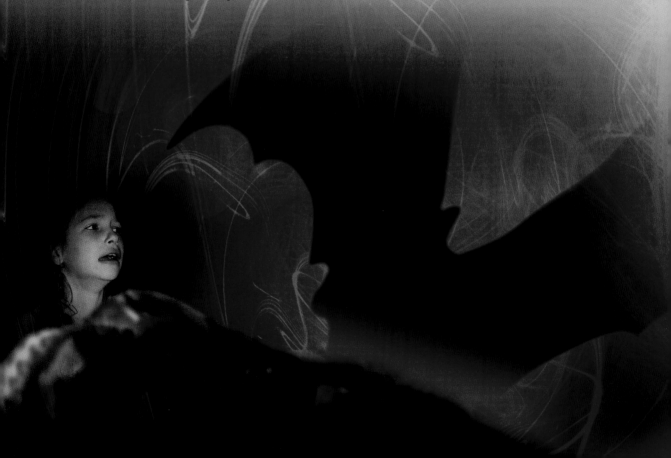

How to End Nightmares

1 **On awakening from a bad dream, think about what was scary in the nightmare and what would make it less scary.**
If, for example, you are falling, think about what would make the fall less dangerous. Could you be falling onto something soft? Could you fall from a lower height? Could someone catch you?

   Similarly, if you are being chased, what would you need to turn and face down your pursuer? Would it be a weapon – a crowbar like Jackie found (see page 105) – or an ally, perhaps a big strong friend? Why not several friends? The more the merrier!

2 **Even though you're thinking about a dream, think realistically.**
For a child, a giant might be a realistic ally, especially a giant he or she is "familiar" with. For an adult, this might not be the case.

   When considering a climbing partner, mountain climbers ask themselves, "would I trust him at the end of a rope?" Think about who you'd trust at the end of a rope. Would it be someone you know, a member of your family, or perhaps a fictional character?

3 **Once you've worked out a way out of the situation, or better, several ways, write the new changed dream down.**
As you do this, enjoy the feeling of turning the tables on your dream adversary(s). Think of how pleased you'll be when this happens in a dream, how excited you'll be that you changed the dream into something positive.

4 **Determine to change the dream in future.**
Decide that the next time you find yourself in this situation in a dream, you'll become aware that you're dreaming and that you'll change it in the way you've determined.

5 **Rehearse your new dream.**
Before going to sleep, rehearse your new dream and go to sleep looking forward to having – and changing – your nightmare.

his dream to help him fight the vampires. When Boobela protested that her friends didn't know how to fight vampires, the head man said they should bring a mirror, because vampires are afraid of mirrors. At this point in the story, my daughter stopped me and looked at me very seriously. "Is that true, Daddy? Are vampires afraid of mirrors?" "First of all," I said, "there are no vampires, except in dreams and stories. But where there are vampires, they're afraid of mirrors because they are terrified of seeing themselves. Some people say that is because they have no reflection." My daughter looked very thoughtful, and this continued until I completed the Boobela story, with her vanquishing the vampires in her dreams with the help of her friends.

That night, the first in a week, I wasn't awoken in the middle of the night by my daughter. In the morning, she awoke with a great big grin. She told me excitedly how Boobela had come into her dream with a giant mirror and three vampires had fled.

She hasn't had a vampire dream since.

Often, children find this way of fighting nightmares comes easily to them. They already live in a world of imagination, and can readily apply it to their dreams. It teaches them a powerful lesson – they don't have to be victims in their own dreams.

THE RISC TECHNIQUE

Rosalind Cartwright developed a technique for changing dreams, similar to the one I use, called the RISC method. It has four main components:

- Recognize during the dream that it is disturbing.
- Identify what has gone wrong.
- Stop whatever is happening.
- Identify the dimensions within which the dream takes place and change negative attributes to positive ones.

Adults can use this technique, too. Jackie, a woman in one of my dream workshops, had recurring dreams in which burglars would break into her house and terrorize her. In the workshop I spoke about the possibility of dream control and my daughter's experience. The following night Jackie had a dream in which thieves broke into her car. She then found a crowbar, beat them up and chased them down the road. Since then, this nightmare has not recurred (with one exception, see page 106).

Crisis Dreaming

Rosalind Cartwright, author of *Crisis Dreaming*, has done research into changing dreams and how this affects your experience during the day. Her particular area of concern was people undergoing a crisis, especially those who had lost a loved one or who had recently divorced. She found that people often felt defeated and depressed after these traumas and that this was reflected in their dreams, in which they were powerless to change distressing situations – they were victims.

She found that if these individuals learned to change their dreams, they recovered much more quickly from the trauma of loss. If they didn't do so, she found that a year later they were still having the same dreams of being a victim, and experiencing the same depression when awake.

Dream Dimensions

One of Cartwright's important contributions is that of applying the notion of dimensions to dreams.

John had a dream in which:

A powerful gorilla charged a group of tourists. I'm one of them. I panicked and ran back toward my car. The rest of the group stood fast and made gorilla noises and actions. The gorilla stopped charging and became interested in their behaviour. I feel chagrined that I ran.

To analyze what dimensions are present in the dream we look at the opposites that are present in the dream. For example in this dream, there are:

- Powerful versus weak
- Safety versus danger
- Frightened versus brave
- Angry versus interested
- Chagrin or shame versus pride

Other common dimensions listed by Cartwright include:

- Old versus young
- Male versus female
- Trust versus mistrust
- Authenticity versus pretense
- Defiance versus compliance
- Independence versus dependence

Cartwright's work showed that the same dimensions are repeated in your dreams over a single night. (She worked in a dream laboratory and so would regularly get accounts of four or five dreams a night by waking people in the middle of each REM period.) She understood this to reflect the way that your dreaming mind struggles to find the right position for you to occupy in relation to a particular dimension of behaviour and thinking.

Changing Nightmares

Ending nightmares is facilitated by the idea of dimensions, as it helps you clarify how and why your dream is a nightmare. Generally, a nightmare is a dream in which you are stuck in the negative side of the dimension in which it takes place. For example, my daughter's dream was one in which she was consistently scared instead of brave, weak instead of strong, and in danger rather than safe. Jackie's dream reflected similar dimensions, along with male versus female.

If Jackie were to use the RISC technique to end her nightmares, she would:

- Recognize when she was feeling scared, weak and in danger.
- Identify that she was allowing what was valuable to her to be taken away.

- Stop this from happening by becoming confident and strong.
- Study the meaning of the dream. The dream showed how Jackie was passive when she was attacked, and that this allowed her valuables to be taken from her all too easily.

In Jackie's case, after a long period in which the nightmare had not recurred, it came back in very particular circumstances. She had ended a relationship but felt impelled to keep a promise she had made before it ended. She took the man to a concert in another city. He had taken advantage of her generosity and had let her drive everywhere. When she returned, she was completely exhausted. Afterwards, she felt she'd been a mug, and had the nightmare where she was "mugged" again.

No Longer a Victim

For some people, just hearing about the possibility of changing their nightmares is enough to help them change them. This is what happened with my daughter and Jackie.

For others, learning to end nightmares takes a bit more work. But it's work well worth doing, as changing your dreams from positive to negative alters the way you think about dreams and yourself.

If you feel (and dream) yourself to be a victim – subject to vampires, muggers or people who criticize or condemn you – learning to change this in dreams can be the first step towards defining yourself in a new and positive way.

Dreams are the ideal place to start this new self-definition. Dreams are idioplastic, shaped by your ideas and desires. As we have already shown, you can experience and behave in new ways for the first time in dreams. For example, people who never cry can find that in a dream they do so for the first time. When you change your nightmares into positive experiences, you take charge of this process.

Ten Minutes to Work with Your Dreams

Most of us don't have enough time. For dream work or anything else. When I say to someone at a party, "I work with dreams," one of the most common responses (apart from "I had this really strange dream …") is, "I'd love to do that! I just don't have time…" Just in case you are using this excuse, I thought I'd nip it in the bud by writing a section on working with dreams when time is extremely limited.

The exercises in this section all take less than 10 minutes. They can be done when you're travelling to or from work, or in any kind of break during the day.

Attitude

It will help if you start by dropping any idea that the aim of your dream work is to understand everything about your dream. You won't, whether you work on it for hours or for minutes.

What are the aims of brief dream work, given that you are not trying to understand your dream completely?

You want:

- To connect with your dream emotionally and intellectually.
- To engage with the issues the dream poses.
- To get beneath the surface of the dream.

These are aims in all dream work. With brief dream work the aim is to do this as quickly as possible and then leave the rest to your unconscious and future dreams.

By engaging briefly with your dream using the techniques in this section, you say to your mind you are interested but you don't have a lot of time. Your mind will respond by popping up insights at odd moments during the day or by advancing your understanding in a future dream. You can facilitate this process by reviewing your dream and the work you've done with it before you go to sleep. Brief dream work is best understood as a way of kick starting a dialogue with your dreams and then continuing the dialogue with minimal effort.

The Big Three in Brief

You can use any of the three basic dream techniques in this chapter to get a quick "take" on a dream. Whichever technique you choose, limit the time involved by working on only one dream image or element. Choose the image carefully. If there's an image that doesn't "fit in" with the dream, choose it. Or choose an element that is unusual or especially vivid, or one that creates a sense of wonder or is disturbing. In other words, choose an image that makes an impact. This will give you the "in" to the dream you need.

Remember our three aims. As you have limited time you can't afford to work mechanically. You're trying to make an emotional or intellectual connection with the image, to stir something up, to get something "cooking".

Cut to the Chase

It's not unusual in the course of a dream group or therapy session to have very limited time to discuss a dream. There is a need to cut to the chase, to get down to what is important quickly. It is this same attitude you'll follow when your time is limited. You will also assume, as we do in all kinds of dream work, that what you come up with, however strange or seemingly unrelated, is important.

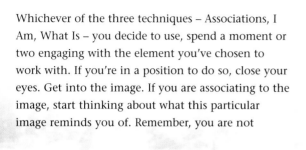

Whichever of the three techniques – Associations, I Am, What Is – you decide to use, spend a moment or two engaging with the element you've chosen to work with. If you're in a position to do so, close your eyes. Get into the image. If you are associating to the image, start thinking about what this particular image reminds you of. Remember, you are not associating to a generic car but to the distinctive car in the dream. Write down your most evocative associations. The number of associations isn't important – three or four will do. What's important is that they connect you with the dream.

If you're using What Is or I Am, often your first thoughts can be discarded. They are part of the "getting into" process. It's the descriptions (in the case of What Is) or the self descriptions (in the case of I Am) that make you think or connect with a feeling that you want to keep. Once again, number isn't important. One or two good descriptions or connections to the image can be enough to start your mind revving. Come back to it later on in the day.

Before you go to sleep, review the dream and the results of your brief dream work. If your work has raised a question for you – put it to your dreams. Then go to sleep.

Part of Me

This exercise is a way of getting at what Jung called the subjective interpretation. Rewrite your dream inserting the words "part of me" after each noun and adjective. A simple dream from Harvey:

A large, fierce black dog was sitting at the bottom of a tree. A scared cat had climbed the tree to get away. They eyed each other. The atmosphere was tense. The cat meowed for help. I heard it and didn't know what to do. The cat jumped onto my head and dug his claws in. I woke up.

Became:

The large, fierce black dog part of me was sitting at the bottom of the tree part of me. The scared cat part of me had climbed the tree to get away. The two parts of me eyed each other. The cat part of me cried for help. The I part of me heard it, and didn't know what to do. The cat part of me jumped on my head and dug its claws in.

In this form, Harvey recognized the dream to be about a conflict within himself. He was working at a large city law firm and was determined to become a partner, almost at any cost (the large fierce black dog part of him). He'd become scared about an ethical compromise he'd felt tempted to make in order to secure his advancement and he wasn't sure he could live with himself afterwards (the scared cat up the tree). The conflict within him was so strong he felt frozen (the two parts eyed each other). He was having nightmares in which he felt extremely guilty (the cat crying for help), but he wasn't willing to help because the prize of becoming a partner was so attractive. However, this painful guilt had got its claws into him and wasn't going to let go – the cat part of himself was going to force him to behave in a way he could live with afterwards.

When-Then

A simple technique from James Hillman's co-author, Patricia Berry, also belongs here. Rewrite your dream making it more general by inserting "when" in front of the first clause of a sentence (or whenever else makes sense), and "then" in front of the second clause (see the example on page 64).

Capitalizing

Another technique from the Hillman chapter can easily be adapted to brief dream work – that of capitalizing the names of characters and actions in your dream. Capitalizing highlights the archetypal aspect of a dream character or action.

Geoff's dream:

A nervous Woody Allen character was in the bedroom with a beautiful girl. He silently gestured to the top left shelf of a high chest of drawers, pointing his fingers like a gun. There was a man in the tiny drawer. They had to kill him.

Capitalized it went:

A Nervous-Woody-Allen character was in the bedroom with A-Beautiful-Woman. He Silently-Gestured to the top left shelf of a High-Chest-of-Drawers, Pointing-with-His-Fingers-Like-a-Gun. There was a Man-in-theTiny-Drawer. They Had-to-Kill-Him.

Geoff felt doing this exercise made the dream more evocative and thought-provoking. After doing it, he found himself wondering during the day who The-Little-Man-in-the Drawer was, and why Woody Allen and A-Beautiful-Woman Had-to-Kill-Him.

Précis the Plot

The last of our time-limited dream exercises comes from Jung's insight that every dream has a dramatic structure. In this exercise, we outline the main plot elements of a dream in order to make its dramatic structure more obvious.

Answer these questions:
• Who is the hero/heroine of the dream?
• What does he/she want? What is their goal in the dream?
• What is stopping the hero/heroine from achieving his/her goal? An obstacle can be internal (a feeling, an inhibition or a thought) or external (a person, physical object or situation).
• How does he/she respond to this obstacle?
• What sets the action going?
• What is the resolution?

7

Sharing Dreams

Dream Groups

"I'll let you be in my dream, if I can be in yours..." Bob Dylan

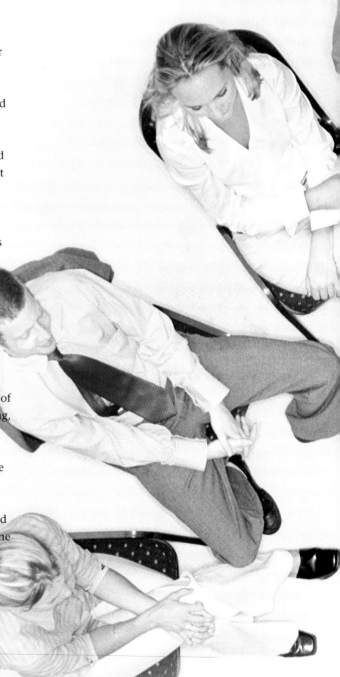

My work with sharing dreams was inspired by an article written by Kilton Stewart, an American psychologist, about a tribe in Malaysia – the Temiar Senoi. Stewart described how every morning the extended Senoi family would share their dreams, starting with the youngest child present. He showed how this practice led to an extremely healthy society. I loved the idea of people sharing their dreams and I was intrigued by the idea that it could have profound effects. By the time I discovered that Stewart had actually made up the morning dream counsel – though not the importance of dreams to the Senoi – I had been running dream groups for many years and had ample evidence of the benefits of sharing dreams.

In this section, I'll talk about my work and the many benefits of sharing your dreams with friends, within couples, and in groups of all kinds. I'll also refer to the work of two other pioneers of dream groups, Montague Ullman and Jeremy Taylor.

Dream Groups

Most work with dreams is based on the experience of sharing dreams in one-to-one therapy or counselling, or on the study by a dreamer of his or her own dreams. Sharing dreams in a group creates a fundamentally different experience and also unique new phenomena.

My dream groups meet once a week. Each meeting has the same simple format – we go around the circle with each person sharing a dream from the week following the last meeting. Doing this means we can assume that the dreams are part of a series, building and commenting on the dreams and discussion of the previous week. Each group lasts two hours. I share dreams and discuss them along with the others in the group.

One of the special features of these groups is that I want people to meet and get to know each other *through* their dreams. So we don't introduce ourselves but instead the first thing we hear from each person is an *initial dream*. We get to know each person through his or her dream and associations, as well as the person's contributions to the discussion of others' dreams. This means that some "facts" that we might consider crucially important about someone – what his or her job or background is, whether the person is single or married, whether he or she has children – may not come up in the group for some time – until a dream "prompts" the person to tell us. This gives the dream group a different "feel". The agenda and self-revelation is governed by the night world.

Which Dream?

How do dreamers decide which dream to tell? Often, people share dreams from either the night after the previous group or the night before the current meeting. These are the dreams most obviously dreamed "for" the group. But dreams can be chosen as being for the group on other criteria, too: they refer explicitly to the dreamer's dreams from the previous week(s); they refer to the discussion of that dream or another in the group; they contain references to group members or the themes of members' dreams; or they're just plain interesting, compelling, nightmarish or recurrent. It's up to each dreamer to make the choice.

But in a group there's also the interesting phenomenon of the dreamer having no choice. It's a story told again and again in different dream groups: early in the week the dreamer has a dream he'd really prefer not to tell – it's too embarrassing, revealing or "silly". Every night before the group he feels increasing pressure to have another dream – so that he doesn't have to tell "that one". By the last night, he's desperate. Still no dream. He is "forced" to tell the dream he didn't want to share – and, of course, it turns out to be hugely helpful.

Out of Your Head, Into the World

It's my policy never to let group members read their dreams. One hundred percent accuracy in reporting the details of a dream is much less important than conveying the spirit of the dream. When you tell a dream, you can get back into it, which enables the group members to possess it as you repossess it.

When you stumble over the scribbled notes from your night's writing, the life of the dream can be completely lost.

To emphasize the wholeness and life of the dream, we don't allow interruptions in its initial telling. The group will have to bear the ambiguities as does the dreamer.

It's in telling your first dream that you come to appreciate what you've done in joining a group. It may be the first time you've ever told a dream seriously to others. (This is because sharing a funny, sexy or scary dream with friends requires a particular tone and is often prefaced by a disclaimer such as "I had a really weird dream …".) Suddenly your dream is no longer in your head, but in the world. Your sharing it has become a way of speaking about yourself or of testifying to the important

relationship between the dream that has been visited upon you and your daily life. It's often in the simple telling of the dream that the dreamer begins to hear resonances in it of which he or she was previously unaware. The distance you work so hard to create when working with your own dreams comes much more easily in a group.

Working with the Dreams

After everyone in the group has shared their dreams, we discuss the dreams as a group. We may choose to divide our time between all the dreams, or to concentrate on one or two.

The dreamer tells his or her dream again, and now the members can ask questions to clarify things that were unclear to them about what happened in the dream and who the dream characters are. For example, if the dream has someone called Mike in it, the group may ask "Who is Mike? What's he like? Who's he to you?".

We then largely use the techniques outlined earlier – Associations, What Is, I Am – to help the dreamer lay out what is implicit in the dream. Often, group members will pick up similarities to earlier dreams the dreamer has told. In a recent group, a member pointed out that the dreamer's previous dream had three mammoths in it, and his current one had three pictures of elephants on the wall. Caught up as he was in the reality of the dreams, the dreamer had missed this striking connection.

If group members have comments and thoughts about the dream, these follow. I urge members to preface their own comments with the phrase (from Jeremy Taylor), "If this were my dream...". This makes clear that their comments come from their own projections and can be as revelatory about their own dreams (and lives) as that of the dream on which they are ostensibly commenting. The ultimate say on the truth of these comments always belongs to the dreamer.

Our priority is to elaborate what the dream means to the dreamer, tracing the connections to his or her day and night worlds to flesh out the dream.

Initial Dreams

Often, the initial dream for a dream group seems to outline a project – an issue the dreamer needs/wants to explore in the group. Such dream projects can include mourning the death of a relationship or parent, celebrating the start of a new relationship, examining a difficult situation at work or with a partner, or exploring one's attitudes (for example, toward spirituality, sex, the unconscious or one's body) in great depth. Being aware of this dream project from the start can make it much easier to understand later dreams in the series.

Initial dreams are always the most difficult to say something sensible about – bear in mind that apart from non-verbal cues (bodily presence, accent, etc.), they may be the only thing we know about the dreamer. If we are sparing in our interpretation of initial dreams, we leave space into which later dreams can grow, thus fleshing out the initial dream imagery.

I often find it useful to assume that these dreams have been dreamed for the group – they're the person's dream world introducing itself. The kinds of questions I will have in my mind include: "What do these dreams reveal about the dreamer's world? Do they define a metaphor, which will be elaborated and explained by later dreams? Do they reveal the dreamer's expectations, anxieties and fears of sharing dreams with strangers?"

The Dream Laboratory

Let's start with a dream fragment, which was all that John, a somewhat uptight and anxious individual, could recall:

I was in a laboratory where they were doing experiments on orange juice. I smelt a very strong smell of jasmine in the laboratory.

John was unable or unwilling to describe more fully the laboratory or the smell of jasmine. Neither could he give any associations to any of the elements – the laboratory, orange juice or jasmine smell. His only comment was that he found the smell very pleasant.

In this dream, John is presented with only one possibility – that of testing – and this only in a rather remote way. He is not to be involved in the testing, but simply finds himself in a place where it will be done. When asked if there might be a parallel between the dream lab and the dream group to whom he was telling it, John drew a blank. Little else was said about this dream. As the dream seemed to show an anxiety about John being experimented on, we felt it best to let it be.

As a general rule, it's important in any dream work to respect resistances. If someone doesn't want to reveal him/herself further, you should stop working with the dream. This resistance can be shown in bodily postures – arms crossed, eyes averted, a voice that becomes inaudible, or a lack of response to suggestions for working on the dream. One thing we have learned from Freud is that there is always a good reason for resistance – usually a fear of some kind. In such cases, my usual practice is to flag up the areas that are unclear. In this dream, I said the meaning of the laboratory, the orange juice and the smell of jasmine were still unclear and I suggested that the dreamer have a future dream about this.

This is exactly what happened. This scant initial dream fragment proved to be the forerunner of a series of future dreams, dreams in which the meaning of the laboratory was elaborated. The following, one of John's later dreams, illustrates the way in which later dreams in a series can shed additional light on misunderstood or partially understood elements of the initial dream.

I was in a laboratory, this time one in which a long metal rod was being tested to ascertain how much tension it could take. A glass ball throwing off sparks appeared miraculously in the air and became a ghostly face. This produced a feeling of overwhelming joy in the people in the laboratory. In the midst of this ecstatic feeling, Mr. Spock from Star Trek *entered the room to say there had been a malfunction in the nuclear power plant and that everyone who had witnessed this apparition had to be decontaminated. After going through the inadequate*

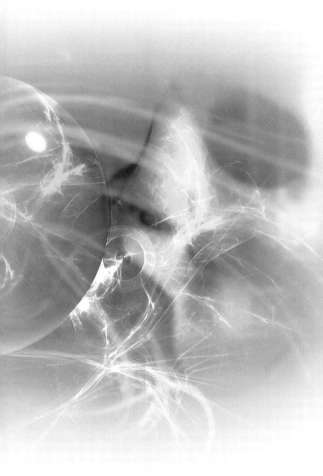

an impersonal and contained dream group – where his metal (mettle) will be tested without disastrous consequences.

A Dream Introduction

The initial dream from Jean, set out below, contains some cultural fears of sharing dreams (as in the dream above) but also serves as a compact and telling dream introduction. It answers the questions of why she has come to the group and what she hopes to get.

I was going to university. Some of the campus was brand new and just being developed. Some of it was quite old. I had a room in the old part. It had very rich wood and was very pleasant. I went downstairs for my interview and I seemed to pass it. On my return, I noticed a section of wall where there were different files. One of them had my name on it and I opened it up. There were references inside and one was from my father. I was just about to read it when something interrupted me.

Then I was in a tower looking down on the campus. I could see that it was quite isolated, especially from the town.

I was in a garden sliding down a chute which I knew to be the kind of chute the Vikings used to sacrifice people – it would split you open. I went down and it didn't hurt. I didn't even get cut, and I was relieved and pleased by this.

There were two final fragments. I was eating a meal with my old nanny there. The food was in tubes and she kept insisting I eat more. It was banana mush – I felt I'd had enough – 1½ tubes.

I left the University room and tried to lock it, but couldn't because the key broke. I tried to hold the key together, but it just wouldn't work.

In Jean's associations to the dream, she said she had gone to a new university, which like the one in the dream, was isolated from the town. The tower looking down on the campus seemed to be a cross between one at the university and the place where the dream group was being held (on the 30th floor of a building). Jean had read somewhere about the

decontamination procedure, I felt I probably would die, but it had been worth it to experience this miracle.

Here we see that something has shifted for John, perhaps as a result of coming to the group. Something new appears in the lab – a ghostly face and overwhelming joy. Soon, however, Mr. Spock, a perfect exemplar of the need to avoid the illogical and irrational, appears to announce that this miracle has been fatally dangerous.

John's initial dream revealed only a laboratory in which orange juice, something usually taken to be healthy, is to be tested in a controlled environment. The later dream reveals why this was felt to be necessary. That which magically appears from nothing (a dream?) is revealed as highly dangerous, the result of the malfunctioning of a "nuclear" plant. This makes clear why John feels the need for

way Vikings had sacrificed victims, but it didn't really fit the image in the dream. She thought this image of the chute that would split you open related to the dream group.

It seemed to embody the fear of having your "insides" painfully and violently exposed to a group of strangers. Interestingly, even in the dream, this fear is shown as unfounded. Another image in the dream that reflects Jean's/our culture's fear of sharing dreams is the last fragment – in which she can't lock the door she has opened to the room/group. The dream genie has been let out of the bottle.

The dream university is also an interesting image, working on many levels. It refers to the university she attended and the dream group she is starting (having an interview for). There is perhaps a wish here for an academic (safe) sort of learning, but already the personal is brought in to the dream – the reference from her father, which she wasn't able to read. An image like this in an initial dream would make me wonder if later dreams in the series might fill in what was in this "reference".

A final image shows Jean being fed banana mush by her old nanny. The fact of having a nanny reveals Jean in a certain light to an English dream group. The dream indicates she is "fed up" with the nanny's world. I would wonder if this was part of what moved her to join a dream group, and helped her to overcome her fear of being exposed.

Settings and Projects

In both examples of initial dreams, the setting of the dream seems to be a cross between the day world the dreamer inhabits and the dream group which he or she is joining. This isn't unusual. It's in elucidating the particular nature of the setting that we begin the work of the group. It's quite a move to join a dream group in our Western culture, in which it is virtually taboo to take dreams seriously. Initial dreams often have something to say about this, expressing wishes or fears about the desire for self-revelation and its converse, the fear of being exposed.

Dream Group Phenomena

So far my description of what happens in dream groups could apply to any one-to-one dream work. But from my very first dream group, I found that many phenomena occur in dream groups that are unusual or unknown in individual dream work or therapy.

It's important to remember that most of my dream groups involve a group of strangers meeting together for a period of roughly eight weeks. Given this, it's remarkable how quickly a group consciousness develops and how it becomes evident in people's dreams. I'll talk here about two manifestations of this consciousness – the development of a shared dream language, and that of a kind of psychic web.

Group Language

The form of a dream group – a circle of people sharing their stories – is similar to that in which an oral tradition is created and shared in non-technological cultures throughout the world. What takes place is not a simple sharing of facts and information but, instead, an imaginative re-possessing of the dream images, which first belonged to one dreamer but now belong to the entire group. As the individual group members listen to the stories, the images in them take hold, seizing their imagination in different ways. They may remind the listeners of their own experiences, dreams they have had, stories they have heard or witnessed.

In each group, these dream characters and environments are defined by their place in the oral tradition. This tradition starts with the first time a character, image or situation appears in a dream. The discussion following this becomes part of the tradition. The following illustrates this process.

In the second week of a dream group, Jane told this dream:

I was in my grandmother's house, in the bedroom. There was a bed in the middle of the room surrounded by newspapers, which entirely covered the floor. The room

was barren and not very pleasant. I decided to explore the rest of the house and started down the stairs. The basement was very clean and well-appointed. In the middle of the room was a bath. I was struck by this but it worked quite well in the room …

Our group discussion highlighted two metaphors, that of the journey into depth (the body? the unconscious?) and of water (see page 64). The first theme was illustrated by the way in which the bedroom (which Jane told us was at the top of the house) was barren, and the floor covered with old newspapers (perhaps indicating Jane found her sex life "old news"). The attractive basement with the bath in the middle suggested something richer down below.

The bath meant different things to people in the group – baptism, cleansing, etc. When doing such a group association, we are not looking for a definite meaning. Rather we are brainstorming, suggesting ideas, which may be fleshed out in future dreams. The following week two different dreamers took up the theme of a descent into the depths and water. Malcolm dreamed:

I was in a building. The top floors were like a warehouse or supermarket. I walked down the stairs and as I went deeper the stairs became more dark and dank, rotten.

Finally I got to the basement. I felt the floor was unsafe and if I walked on it I might fall through to the water, which I knew ran underneath. I went back up the stairs but there was a group of people coming down, some singly, some in small groups. I felt left out.

Then I was at the door of the basement. Somehow I had crossed it. The door opened onto a swimming pool, next to the bank of a river. I was at the top. Somebody asked, "Do you want to go swimming in the Thames?" I said, "No, it's too dirty." Then I noticed there was a Statue of Liberty in the middle of the Thames, spouting chlorinated water. I said, "I think it's too cold."

Rosie dreamed:

I was in the restaurant where I work. I started going down these stairs to the toilet. I got to a very deep level where there was a sandstone cavern. The walls were dirty and there were pipes that were dripping. There was dirty water and cigarette butts on the floor. The place had been spoiled by the people there before.

I went up a couple of stairs and came upon a man who was sitting at a table. He asked if I could bring him a meal there. At first, I thought, "How could anyone want to eat in this place?" Then I looked around and saw that the sandstone was clean and there was light coming in from the side. It wasn't unpleasant.

I told him I couldn't really do that. He didn't seem to understand about the practical side of things – like he might leave without paying his bill … Then I said, "You can go upstairs, get some food and then bring it down here if you wish."

In both these dreams we see a reworking and elaboration of the basic metaphors in Jane's dream. The visit to a deeper level (emotions/the body? the unconscious? dreams?) is repeated, but in each case in an entirely individual way.

Both dreams employ humour to make their point. When Malcolm demurs at swimming in the dream river because it's too "dirty", a chlorine-spouting Statue of Liberty appears as if to say your fear is groundless, the water's fine. But he still balks. In Rosie's dream, her incredulity that anyone would want to eat (find nourishment) in the depths was answered by another look showing it wasn't such an odd idea. Still, she can't bear to take food there.

Both dreams provide new takes on the metaphor of exploring the depths and both differently portray the surface/day world and that which lies beneath it. The elaboration, enrichment and particularization of

dream imagery is essential to the development of an image vocabulary in a group. It illuminates both the general meaning of a metaphor and the particular meaning it has for the dreamer.

Simone's dream occurred two weeks after those outlined above:

I was in Greece for a holiday with a group of people I didn't like, people from school. I went my separate way to practice swimming with my instructor, and as the dream went on, I got better and better at swimming.

Then it was the end of the holiday and I had to return to the group. Instead of walking, I decided to swim across a very beautiful, very deep, very blue bay. It was an amazing experience. I was alternately swimming then flying over the water, then swimming again. I had no trouble swimming the entire length of the bay.

Simone told us that normally she was frightened of swimming out of her depth (an interesting expression in the light of the dream series). Her dream shows a different relationship with water than that of the other dreamers. In it, the experience of working with her instructor enables her to feel at home in the water, and she is able to master her fear in a joyous finale. This may well be a comment on her experience in the group.

Rachel had found the group frustrating because she had been unable to remember many dreams during it. She told the following dream during the group's last meeting:

I was in a room filled with baths, though they looked like industrial tanks. I would get into one, then would spring (or be ejected) into the air, then would get into it again, and would be ejected again.

Then I was holding a newspaper, worrying about the possibility of nuclear war. I felt that in some way the sides would come together. I wasn't sure what that way was or what it would result in, but I was sure it was in the newspaper. I woke up worried it would not happen.

There was much laughter during the telling of Rachel's dream, partly because its meaning seemed so obvious given the oral tradition in the group and her experience of it. In the dream, baths, newspapers and water were all combined to make a statement about her frustration in the group, her fear, which might have led to her difficulty remembering dreams, and her feeling that the answer was in the newspaper, a reference to the newspapers which covered the floor in Jane's initial dream.

Given its context, this dream hardly needed any interpretation as the laughter during its telling indicated. The new thing it brings to the party is the fear of "nuclear war" and the hope that the "two sides would come together". These were explored in the discussion following the dream. Rachel felt the two sides that needed to come together were her emotional and her intellectual, her earth and water, her dream and day "sides".

The Web of Consciousness

One of the most striking things in dream groups is the way that two kinds of coincidences occur: those in dreams told on the same night (and dreamed between the group's meetings) and those between the content of people's dreams and real-life events (of which they were completely unconscious) in the lives of other group members. In both cases, the dreams are told without any awareness (from the dreamer) that such a coincidence has occurred. For me, these coincidences demonstrate vividly how quickly a dream group forms a group consciousness, in which its members are in "contact" with one another not only in the group, but in the time between sessions. The following four dreams, which were were told on the same night, illustrate the phenomena. The coincidences between dreams are highlighted in grey.

James's dream (November 4th, afternoon):

I was in a dark tunnel … A train was coming towards me … I found myself in the driver's cabin. He was a black man, standing at the wheel. I hoped he wouldn't notice me, then I left the cabin through swing doors, like those in a hospital … I found myself on the deck of a boat *in darkness. The black man had been the captain. I*

thought back to the tunnel and how it was impossible to have a train in such a small space. I realized I must have been dreaming and that I was still dreaming. *I remembered Joe said I shouldn't get too excited; otherwise I would wake up, so I curled my fingers up and looked through them. If I saw anything too exciting, I'd bunch them up again and block it from view.* I took my hand away and found myself in a park by *a swimming pool. Old people were sitting on the grass … On the right was a young girl, she was my mother. On the left was my girlfriend standing in a striped swimsuit.*

Joe's dream (November 3rd/4th):

In a lobby of a hotel. I was talking to my father. The lobby was packed with people. I urged my father to go swimming. He wanted to see my mother in her swimming suit first. My mother's friend who had had a sex change operation was there with her.

I had a standby ticket to fly on an airplane to Israel. I then seemed to be on the plane and it had already taken off. I could see the scenery moving. Now the plane seemed to have become the QE2 …

On waking, I had an association to the scenery outside the airplane – it reminded me of a dream in which James had been lucid, and it made me wonder briefly if there would prove to be some connection with James' dream that week.

Annie's dream (November 3rd/4th):

I went to the Galleria … It looked different. Phillip said, "Have you got your driving licence now?" which was an absurd thing to say. Bill was wearing a long outfit – a long striped dress, a bit tatty and red women's shoes. He didn't look like in drag, just a bit weird.

Thomas's dream (November 2nd/3rd):

I was leaving the Marquee after seeing a group. In the street in my car I sit in the back. Roosevelt (a mutual black friend) arrived and I let him drive my car. Almost immediately, I decided he shouldn't be driving, so I lean forward shouting "Stop. Stop"….

Thomas's association to this dream was that he had

DREAM GROUP COINCIDENCES CHART

James	Joe	Annie	Thomas
November 4 afternoon	November 3/4	November 3/4	November 2/3
In cabin of train with a mysterious black driver	DR: George called me during the week		In car, with George as a driver
Train changed into ocean liner	Airplane changed into QE2		
I went through some swing-type doors, the kind in a hospital	DR: I was actually in a hospital at the time of the dream, or just before it		
Tracer: Joe tells me not to get too excited.	Tracer: On awakening, scene outside the airplane reminds me of James' previous lucid dream		
Girlfriend in black and purple striped bikini	My mother in green and white striped swimming suit	Tom wearing long striped dress	
Swimming pool	I urge my father to go swimming		
	Mother's friend had a sex change operation	Bill was wearing a dress and red women's shoes	
		Phillip asked if I had a driver's licence	DR: I was thinking of giving people driving lessons
	DR: George called me to talk about ways to make money		DR: I was thinking of ways to make money
Using hand to control lucid dream	DR: Peter and I had spoken about this aspect of lucid dreams		

COINCIDENCE?

In trying to assess dream coincidences, you need to look at whether they have been prompted by earlier dreams, discussions in the group, or by contacts between group members during the week. Finally, you need to look at events in the news. (Obviously if an elephant is on the front page of all the daily papers and several people have dreams about elephants, the coincidence between dreams is easily explained.) You also need to look at the specificity of the coincidence – if two people dream of houses, that is hardly very striking, but if both houses are painted blue and have bright orange windows then that is clearly much more indicative of some kind of extra-sensory contact.

None of us could recall any references in the group to driving licences or lessons, stripy dresses or swimsuits, sex-change operations or transvestites, trains or planes changing into ships (or ships at all), or swimming pools. We had talked about lucid dreams and tracer elements, conversations prompted by earlier dreams in the group. None of the members of the group had any contact with one another during the week. Roosevelt, a mutual friend, had contacted me, but not Thomas.

Having seen such coincidences in many dream groups, often

been thinking of ways to make money and one idea he'd had was to give driving lessons.

The coincidences between the dreams and the connections with the lives of others in the dream group are outlined in the box, opposite. Two terms require explanation: DR refers to day residue (something that actually happened), and a tracer is an element in a dream that acts as a signal to you that some part of the dream is psychic (generally on awakening). I'll talk more about this concept on page 148.

Dream/Day Replay

Another example of group phenomena is a dream/day replay. This is when someone tells a dream and unconsciously repeats his or her dream actions in the group. Robert, a group trainer and therapist, told the following dream:

I was in a group and someone in it said I was like a person called Sal, who I'll tell you about later. Everyone in the group laughed in a kind of recognition. I didn't like this comparison and wanted to confront the person who said it. I stared at him but he just stared back at me. I realized I wasn't in a very good position to confront him

given the way the group felt.

After telling the dream, Robert said that Sal was a member of a group he was running, and that they weren't at all alike. The very idea that anyone could think he bore any resemblance to another made him furious in the dream, and even now he found it seriously annoying.

Someone asked Robert if he could characterize Sal for us. "He's not at all like me," he assured us. "He's short and dark with a beard, very intense and very paranoid." At this description, everyone in the group started to laugh as they realized that Robert – a short, dark man with a beard – was just a little bit like Sal. Robert protested he really wasn't like Sal; he wasn't as paranoid and as quick to be angry. The laughter intensified.

Eventually, Robert was forced to concede that he wasn't going to convince anyone he wasn't like Sal. He admitted that he and Sal had more in common than he had allowed himself to think, and this was the reason he had such a problem with him being in the group.

accompanied by tracer elements, I do not believe they happen through chance alone. Examples such as the ones illustrated here are just too strong and too specific to be simply explained away as pure chance.

For me, such coincidences are manifestations of the level of intimacy and connection that participation in a dream group engenders. When the participants of a group are open to such phenomena, they can become

part of the currency of the group, testifying to the way that dreams and our consciousness transcend our ordinary understanding of space and time.

It's important to remember that apart from the tracer elements in two of the dreams, none of the dreamers were at all aware that their dreams were in any way "psychic". We would never have discovered the dream coincidences had we not

shared and discussed them. This can't help but make me wonder if such psychic phenomena are common in dreams, but that we simply don't ever find out about them because we forget most dreams, and share few of the ones we do remember.

Your Own Dream Partner or Group

Sharing dreams with sympathetic others who are on the same wavelength is often a joy and a revelation. Even after working with my own dreams for many years in a variety of contexts, I find sharing dreams in a group helps me make connections which, on reflection, were obvious but that I somehow missed on my own.

Below, I explain how to share dreams with a partner and start a dream group of your own. But first a warning: I said *sympathetic others*, not sharing dreams with any Tom, Dick or Harry. Dreams are enormously intimate expressions of your being. Most of us have a sense of this, and so are naturally reticent about sharing a dream unless it feels "safe" to do so. Many of the guidelines here for sharing dreams are aimed at ensuring that sense of safety.

Sensitivity and Secrets

It's important in any dream sharing, whether with a partner or a group, to be sensitive to the fact that dreamers may reveal much more than they intend when telling a dream. Closely-held secrets can "pop out" from dreams that were thought to be entirely innocent. It's important to be sensitive to this possibility, and if such secrets (lies, miscarriages, affairs, for example) do come out, to tread carefully in relation to them. As ever, the dreamer must be the judge of how far he or she wishes to go in exploring the dream and what it reveals.

Dream Appreciation

Montague Ullman, a dream group pioneer, has proposed that we replace the notion of dream interpretation with that of dream appreciation, especially for work outside the clinical setting. This has many advantages. It frees us from needing to have the "final word" on the dream. It's also very much in accord with my emphasis on keeping the dream alive and respecting its integrity. When you appreciate a dream on some of its many levels of meaning, you enrich your experience of it, and consequently your own life. You are then in a better position to address your own difficulties from a position of knowledge and sympathetic understanding. This should be the aim of all your dream work.

General Guidelines

When sharing dreams with either a dream partner or a group, several rules need to be respected:

- Confidentiality. Speaking about dreams is intimate, and intimate disclosures are part of the currency of dream sharing. Everyone needs to understand that disclosures must be kept within the group or partnership. This can be overridden only with the dreamer's explicit agreement.
- Authority. All decisions about whether to share a dream or how far to work with it belong to the dreamer alone. There should be no pressure or subtle bullying applied to force a dreamer to go beyond his or her comfort zone. If this guideline is respected, then over time, one's comfort zone will increase.
- Meaning. The dream ultimately means what makes sense to the dreamer. If others have different opinions, that is part of the rich tapestry of life. Any attempt to force a meaning on a dreamer must be completely discouraged.

Partner Guidelines

1 Try to meet for a minimum time – say 45 minutes. (Catch up briefly or otherwise it will eat into the time for sharing dreams. Gossip and general chat come after you've shared dreams, if there's time.)

2 Decide how much time you have. Divide the available time between you and stick to this division however interesting your enquiries. Both of you are responsible for time keeping.

3 When you share dreams, commit to doing nothing else at the same time. Neither of you will be washing dishes, sorting laundry, reading a newspaper, eating, etc.

4 Take a quiet moment to centre yourselves before starting.

5 In each person's division of time aim to:
  • Share a dream or two.
  • Clarify the dream with questions from the partner ("Who's Jake? What was the house like?").
  • Give associations to the dream. This can be directed by dreamer or partner. The partner can use the *If this were my dream* format to give suggestions as to possible meanings.
  • Use the *I Am* or *What Is* techniques to get further into the dream elements. This can be directed by the partner or the dreamer.
  • Have the dreamer sum up what he or she has learned. If the partner feels this is not "new", press the dreamer to say what new message the dream brings.

6 Close the session in a formal way, perhaps with thanks and an arrangement for the next time to meet.

Finding a Dream Partner

You get the most out of sharing dreams if you do it regularly. Keep this in mind when choosing someone to be your dream partner. Other factors to consider are:

• Is this someone with whom you feel comfortable? Someone you trust?
• Do you feel "judged" by him or her? Are you in competition with each other?
• Do you share similar values? Interests?
• Is he or she defensive? Does the person make you feel defensive?

Choosing a dream partner isn't an "intellectual" decision. Consider all of the above but also pay special attention to your gut instinct. Does it feel right to you?

Commitment

Once you've chosen someone to share your dreams with (and vice versa, of course), discuss the guidelines for sharing dreams (see box, left) and either agree to them, or amend them and agree the amendments. It's not these particular rules that are important – it's agreement on a way of proceeding that suits you both. Perhaps you'd like to formally "incorporate" your dream partnership by literally signing up to a set of guidelines. Once you've done this, both of you are responsible for making sure they are kept to.

Dream Groups

For rough classification purposes, dream groups fall into two categories: those that are based on the notion that dream language is a universal vocabulary with some elements particular to the dreamer, and those who believe the vocabulary of dreams is quite specific to the dreamer with some universal elements. Montague Ullman belongs to the first group, I belong to the second. These assumptions produce very different kinds of dream groups, and very different kinds of dreams.

My experience of trying to run an "Ullman" group was that it never really gelled for me or the participants, perhaps because of my different

The Ullman Dream Group

Montague Ullman's *Working with Dreams* is an invaluable guide for starting a dream group based on the assumption that dream language is in some way universal. An Ullman group has the following format:

1   The group is asked who had a dream that can be shared and worked with.

2   The dream is shared, with the rest of the group listening and taking notes.

3   The group asks questions to clarify the content of the dream.

4   Everyone is asked to feel the dream as his or her own and to say what it makes them feel. The dreamer listens.

5   The group is asked to own the images in the dream. If they were your images, what would they suggest? (The aim here is to give the dreamer a fund of meanings to draw on.) The dreamer listens.

6   The dreamer is asked what recent events may have inspired the dream, and what connections he or she makes with the feelings and imagery of the group. The group leader orchestrates this process, which might include further interjections from the group.

experience and assumptions. Given this, I would suggest that new groups need to discuss which way of working makes more sense to them or, even better, to try both.

Where to Find Your Group

If you live in an area where you think such groups already exist, you'll need to give a thought to where you might find them. Some ideas: Google your local area for "dream group". If there are growth or human development centres, they may be able to help. Try advertising your desire to join a dream group on local bulletin boards.

For most people, however, the only way to participate in a dream group is to start one yourself. I'll be assuming this is what you're going to do. In this context, finding your group means recruiting its members.

Before you think about who to approach or how to advertise, think about the values and experiences you'd most like your group to share. Becoming clear on this will shape your search. Are there any friends, colleagues or acquaintances you'd like to ask? Start with them. They may well have other contacts.

Put up a notice in appropriate places. Some possibilities are local health food stores; growth, yoga or Pilates centres; places of worship and community centres.

When people respond, don't feel you have to convince them to join. Instead, check out if the other people want similar things, what their experiences are, whether you "click" in any way. Will the others be willing to make the time commitment necessary? Ideally, a dream group would meet once a week at the beginning, but fortnightly might be the best you can manage.

Aim to have from three to eight members in your initial group.

What You Do

I give formats for two different kinds of dream groups in the accompanying boxes – ones that assume dreams are part of a universal language (Ullman) and ones that assume dreams are unique to the person (Dream Circle). But other possibilities exist; Jeremy Taylor (another group pioneer), for example, runs groups that combine elements of both – all the members of the group share a dream, and then one or two dreams are worked with extensively using techniques similar to Ullman's. The best advice I can give is to experiment and see what works best for your group.

What You'll Learn

The beauty of dream groups is that you don't only learn when your dream is being worked on. Every dream you hear and imaginatively possess will teach you something. And you will also learn a great deal about how you see things from what you notice in other people's dreams. The *If this were my dream …* format makes it clear that your suggestions are yours and may be as illuminating about your psychology as about the dreamer's. Over the course of the group you'll come to realize that some people specialize in word play while others in issues to do with power, relationships or the body. Clearly, people who see things in terms of power dynamics will be sensitive to this issue in others, as will those who prioritize relationships, etc.

For most people, a dream group becomes one of the highlights of their week, a place where they can get to know themselves and others in an honest, intimate, exciting way.

The Dream Circle

This assumes that only the dreamer can know what his or her particular imagery means, though the group can help by giving its own ideas and understandings.

1   Either the group starts with a brief check-in, in which case someone is responsible for keeping it short, or there may be a moment of silence for the group members to concentrate on how they're feeling, and to separate themselves from the hustle and bustle of daily life.

2   One by one, the group members share a dream they've had since the last group meeting. This is done without comment by the other members.

3   After this is done, a group has two options: It can work briefly with each dream in turn, dividing the available time by the number of participants, or it can ask who wants to work with a dream, and work with this dream at greater length. (This may mean that not everyone gets his or her dream discussed each week.) Whichever option is chosen, the way of working with the dream is the same.

4   The dreamer retells the dream.

5   The group asks questions to clarify the content of the dream.

6   The group helps the dreamer clarify individual elements of the dream, by using the *What Is* or *I Am* techniques.

7   Group members and the dreamer work together to make sense of the dream. When members make suggestions as to the meaning, ideally they precede their constructions with *If this were my dream….*

8

Lucid Dreaming

A World of Possibilities

Lucid dreams are dreams in which you are conscious that you are dreaming. Put like that, they sound like an intellectual curiosity. Usually you're not conscious that you're dreaming, sometimes you are. Big deal.

The big deal is the extraordinary effect that becoming conscious has on the experience of dreaming. It's as if the vividness knob is being turned up to 11. Colours are brighter, sounds and smells more intense. Often the dream assumes a preternaturally real quality.

And that's just for starters. The fact that you are conscious means that you can take control of your dream. You can fly, visit friends and practice sports or other tasks that you want to improve. You can sleep with movie stars or dispel nightmares from within the dream. You can change your dream world at a whim, and all this with a profound sense of reality. You can even have numinous and ecstatic experiences of the divine. In other words, becoming conscious that you're dreaming creates enormous possibilities, some of which can only occur when you're dreaming.

And this would be quite wonderful enough if it was all. But there is evidence that what you do in lucid dreams has real effects in the day world – on your physical body and that of others, on other's dreams and on your predispositions to react.

The Historical Record

Lucid dreams have been a part of human experience from before Christ. "For often", wrote Aristotle, "when one is asleep, there is something in

FREQUENTLY ASKED QUESTIONS

Is lucid dreaming dangerous?
For most people, lucid dreams are an enormously pleasurable and positive experience. Part of the pleasure is that a person's awareness enables him or her to change unpleasant situations into positive ones.

I feel dreams are a message from my unconscious mind or a higher self. Wouldn't becoming lucid and changing dreams interfere with this?

I, too, believe that dreams contain great wisdom and are a valuable source of counsel. However, even the most prolific lucid dreamers have only three or four lucid dreams a week, Ithat leaves over 30 unaltered dreams.

The notion that using your consciousness to alter dreams is "interference" also needs to be questioned. We don't think it "meddling" when we use our awareness to avoid an accident or choose the best path for our future.

Consciousness is an enormous human achievement and using it can hardly be considered "interference"!

You've spent a big section of the book showing me how to work with my dreams to understand their meanings. Isn't lucid dreaming opposed to this?
In dreaming as in life, "for everything there is a season". To paraphrase Ecclesiastes: a time to act and a time to symbolize, a time to experiment

consciousness which declares that what then presents itself is but a dream."

In the late nineteeth century, remarkable books on lucid dream experimentation were produced by the Marquis d'Hervey de Saint-Denys and Frederik Willems van Eeden. Both these writers, and others such as Oliver Fox, were interested in how you develop the capacity to have lucid dreams or as Saint-Denys put it, how to guide dreams consciously. Now, thanks to the technology of modern dream laboratories and the work of dedicated oneironauts (dream explorers) such as Stephen LaBerge, Paul Tholey and Alan Worsley, we know a great deal about what is possible in a lucid dream, what is happening in our brains when we have such dreams, and the effects that lucid dreams can produce in the "real world". We also have tried-and-tested methods for helping everyone develop the capacity to have regular lucid dreams.

Lucid Dreams in the Lab

How do you communicate from within a dream that you are conscious when you can't move your body due to dream paralysis? For many years lucid dreamers could not figure out how to overcome this obstacle, which left most scientists skeptical of the idea of lucidity.

Then, in 1975, two people in different places came up with the same answer. Keith Hearne, an English researcher, found that Alan Worsley, a lucid dreamer, could signal that he was lucid by moving his eyes left then right eight times in a row. This signal was clearly visible in the polygraph recording of the dream. The same eye-signalling technique was discovered by Stephen LaBerge in America.

From these and other experiments we now know that lucid dreams occur during REM periods and are real dreams. The later the REM cycle in the night, the more chance you will have a lucid dream.

I have previously discussed how real dreams appear to the body. Lucid dreamers have confirmed and extended these results. In particular, Stephen LaBerge and his team of dream researchers at Stanford University have been able to confirm many of our suspicions about the reality of dreams.

We know that when a typical right hander is

and a time to provide food for interpretation. In lucid dreaming, we flex our consciousness and action muscles. We enjoy, we change the environment, we actively encounter difficulties aware of what we are doing. We agree that all this is an important and valid part of life. Why not of dreams?

As we work with dreams, we find that dreams "want" different things from us. Some dreams "beg" for interpretation. Others ask simply to be lived fully.

I am not saying that lucid dreams (or lucid life) can't bear reflection. The sheer fact that we are lucid in a dream can serve to highlight our dream (and waking) behaviour. For example, when we don't do or say what we want for fear of what other dream characters will think of us, or when we shy away from a dream confrontation to avoid trouble. Why act like this when you know you are in a dream? Do you act like this when awake also?

My lucid dreams feel so real. Is it possible that I am interacting with someone else who is also dreaming?
We are just beginning to explore what is possible in lucid dreams and how true to life they can be. See the examples on pages 136 and 153.

(This box is partially based on questions and answers from LaBerge's *Exploring the World of Lucid Dreaming*.)

awake and singing his or her right cerebral hemisphere is activated, and that counting activates the left cerebral hemisphere. LaBerge and his team thought "Why not get lucid dreamers to signal they are dreaming, sing in their dreams, and then signal when they are finished singing?" This is exactly what they did. On the EEG machine, the dreamers' brains registered increased right cerebral activity. When the dreamers counted in their dreams, activity in their left cerebral hemispheres went up.

This kind of experiment showed that the activities that we engage in during lucid dreams happen in real time. Of course, we can have dreams that seem to last much longer than the hour that our longest dream takes. It's probable that this phenomenon is accomplished in the same way as in movies, by jump cutting between different events.

LaBerge's lucid dreamers also experimented with breathing. When they became lucid they gave a signal, and then either held their breaths or breathed rapidly, as previously agreed. Again, their "real" breathing accompanied their dream breathing.

Sex in Lucid Dreams

Many lucid dreamers describe having intense orgasmic sex in lucid dreams. LaBerge was determined to test this in the laboratory, too. One of his usual subjects, "Miranda", regularly experienced dream sex. LaBerge brought her into the laboratory and recorded 16 channels of physiological data. Miranda agreed to signal the start of her lucid dream, the start of sexual activity, the actual moment of orgasm, and her waking from the dream. The experiment was a total success. Miranda had a three-minute lucid dream in which she did all the above. Quoting LaBerge from his *Lucid Dreaming*:

…she suspected she was dreaming, and tested her state by flying to float into the air. As soon as she found herself floating, she was convinced she was dreaming and made the agreed-upon signal as she floated through her bedroom wall … Continuing to fly, she found herself over a campus resembling both Oxford and Stanford. She flew through the cool evening air, free as a cloud … After

a few minutes, however, she decided it was time to begin the experiment. Flying through an archway, she spotted a group of people – apparently visitors touring the campus. Swooping down to the group, she picked the first man within reach. She tapped him on the shoulder, and he came towards her as if knowing exactly what he was expected to do. At this she signalled again, marking the beginning of sexual activity. She says that she must have already been excited from the flying, because after only 15 seconds she felt as if she were about to climax. She signalled a third time, marking her experience of orgasm as the final waves began to die down. Shortly after this she let herself wake up, and signalled, according to plan, as soon as she felt herself back in bed. She said the dream orgasm had been neither long nor intense, but was quite definitely a real orgasm.

Looking at the physiological measures accompanying the dream, LaBerge found the graph of vaginal blood flow corresponded with every particular of Miranda's lucid dream report. During the time between her second and third signals, when she was having intercourse in the dream:

Her respiration rate, vaginal muscle activity and vaginal blood flow all reached their highest levels of the night … The increases in respiration rate and vaginal blood flow are fully comparable to those typically observed during waking orgasm – and the lucid dream orgasm was described as being "not very strong"!

The same precise correspondence was found with a male subject in a similar laboratory experiment, including the increased respiratory rate.

While having sex in dreams is one of the ordinary pleasures of dreaming, sex in lucid dreams is different, in both its vividness and the element of choice it offers. This experiment shows that it provides the same release as "real" sex.

How to Become Lucid in Your Dreams

The good news is that you're already halfway there. By this point in the book you will have already learned to remember your dreams regularly and in detail, how to awaken your dream senses and to set up dreams before you go to sleep.

You may already have had a lucid dream or at least a dream in which you wondered if you were dreaming. It may have been a dream in which you woke yourself up or reassured yourself that you were having a dream. Even if you have not achieved this kind of pre-lucid state, the capacity to remember dreams regularly means that on some level you're already aware that you're dreaming and use this to wake yourself up during an REM period.

Having a lucid dream means using this awareness to wake up your consciousness during a dream rather than wake up completely. It is a skill that can definitely be learned. The steps are:

1   Question that you are dreaming during a dream.
2   Answer the question affirmatively.
3   Deal with the shock of attaining lucidity (and the accompanying joy and increase in vividness) without waking.
4   Maintain the lucid state and use it to do what you want.

In this section, I will help you achieve the first three steps, and give you several techniques for inducing lucid dreams. In the next section, I'll help you learn how to maintain your lucid state and to experiment with it.

Setting Up a Lucid Dream

These techniques are ones that I have taught others and used successfully for more than 20 years. The basic technique is an extension of the one I've already mentioned several times – before you go to sleep, concentrate on your desire to have a lucid dream. Repeat to yourself, "Tonight I'll become conscious during a dream" (or use another form of words based on the models in *How to Remember Dreams*, see page 12.) Picture yourself vividly aware in a dream that you are dreaming, full of the accompanying joy and intensity. Keep bringing yourself back to your intention as you drift off to sleep.

There are two ways you can make this basic technique more powerful.

First, look over your dream diary before going to sleep. Become aware of common elements of your recent dreams. Have you been dreaming of a particular friend or a particular place – your house, your office? Is there an activity you perform regularly in a dream – do you study, play tennis, drive in a car? Has there been a common theme? In particular, try to pick out anything that can serve as a trigger to remind yourself that you are dreaming.

1   Make a list of the elements that recur regularly.
2   Ask yourself, which of these will most likely recur tonight?
3   Add to the instructions above, "If I dream about X, I will become aware that I am dreaming." Then vividly picture this happening – you see or do X in a dream, and you suddenly know that you are dreaming.

Second, decide you will dream about something in particular, and that this thing will trigger your awareness that you are dreaming. In my early lucid dreams, I used a technique from books by Carlos Castenada – before I went to sleep I'd suggest to myself that while I was dreaming I'd find myself looking at my hand and that this would trigger my awareness that I was dreaming.

All Through the Night

Remember that you are much more likely to have a lucid dream later in the dream cycle. Stephen LaBerge's MILD (Mnemonic Induction of Lucid Dreams) technique aims to enable you to create consciousness in your last dreams before waking, ideally the dreams after dawn. (This exercise is taken from his invaluable *Exploring the World of Lucid Dreaming*).

You use the MILD technique (below) in the middle of the night. As it requires you to wake up for an extended period, it is best to experiment with it on weekends and holidays.

1 Remember a dream during the night, in as much detail as possible. Wake up fully to do this. For the best results, stay awake for 30–60 minutes
2 Focus on setting up a lucid dream. Tell yourself, "Next time I'm dreaming I want to remember I'm dreaming." Keep bringing your attention back to this thought.
3 See yourself becoming lucid. At the same time, imagine yourself back in the dream you've just remembered. Think of particular points in the dream and imagine using them as triggers to awaken your consciousness. For example, if your previous dream involved a friend, Sally, recall the dream, think of Sally and imagine yourself becoming lucid at the sight of her. Do the same with other elements of the dream.
4 Alternate steps 2 and 3 until your intention is clear.
5 Drift off to sleep as you do this.

Practice Makes Lucid

Simply reading about the above techniques is unlikely to produce a lucid dream. You'll have to practice. My basic technique can be practiced every night. If you do this, expect it to take between a week and a month to have your first lucid dream. The ability to have lucid dreams at will is relatively difficult to accomplish – certainly much more difficult that having problem-solving dreams. But for a dedicated oneironaut, the result is well worth the effort. Just as a basis for comparison, LaBerge, who was writing a PhD thesis on lucid dreaming and was thus highly motivated, increased his personal rate of lucid dreams from one a month to three or four a week over several years.

The Critical Faculty

Using the techniques above may well bring about a direct transition to lucidity during a dream. But for many people, there is an intermediate step. During a dream, they start to wonder whether they are dreaming.

For these people, the key is to becoming lucid is developing the critical faculty (a phrase coined by Oliver Fox, an early lucid dreamer). The critical faculty enables us to:

• Question whether we are dreaming,
• Test our dream state,
• Overcome rationalizations of dream phenomena and
• Decide that this is indeed a dream.

Many of us have had the experience of dreaming, and of reminding ourselves, or someone saying to us, this is only a dream. We think nothing of it. Neither do we think anything of the way a dream character/building/scene/atmosphere can change in a moment, the way an elephant or obelisk fits in our bedroom, the way we can meet someone with wings or two heads.

If we develop our critical faculty, every moment of oddity in a dream can awaken us to the fact that we are dreaming. We can think, "Wait a second, Tom was wearing a blue suit and now he's wearing pink swimming trunks! I wonder if this is a dream?" We do a state test, overcome the rationalizations ("He's probably just started a holiday!"), and then realize we are dreaming.

Asking the Question

How can we come to question that we are dreaming during a dream? One way is to start asking the question when we are awake. This method, used by experienced lucid dreamers Stephen LaBerge and Paul Tholey (a German psychologist), is a development of Eastern enlightenment techniques.

Simply put, you make it a discipline to ask yourself "Am I dreaming?" at least 10 times a day. After you ask it, you seriously look around and examine the environment, perhaps performing some of the state tests given in the box opposite. For it to work, you have to do this seriously, however foolish it makes you feel. If you simply answer "Of course I'm not dreaming!" you'll do the same in your dream.

Testing the Dream State

Once you are able to ask the question, "Am I dreaming?" you need to be able to give the correct answer. Sometimes this is straightforward. Something happens that triggers your critical faculty, and you immediately jump to the conclusion that you're dreaming. But more often, the sheer reality of the dream makes it difficult to tell whether you're dreaming or awake. In the box opposite, there are seven tests you can ask yourself in your dream. Memorize one or two that seem most likely to be useful to you, and remind yourself of them before you go to sleep.

False Awakenings

A false awakening occurs when you dream you've awoken and start to do your usual waking activities, when suddenly you realize you're still asleep and dreaming. Such awakenings can occur from ordinary dreams but are much more common (and convincing) from lucid dreams.

I've had such false awakenings from lucid dreams, dreamed I was very excited at having the dream, and then either dreamed I was recording it, or analyzing and interpreting it. Then I start to wonder whether I'm still dreaming. In this situation, do a state test, and launch another lucid dream.

State Tests

(following suggestions by Keith Hearne and Stephen LaBerge)

1. Switch on an electric light in the dream. If it doesn't work or there is a malfunction of any kind – i.e. there are no switches – you're dreaming.

2. Attempt to "fly" or "float" in mid-air. If you can, you're dreaming.

3. Jump off an object such as a chair. If you descend slowly, you're dreaming.

4. Find some writing. Read it once, look away and then read it again. If the text has changed, if you can't read it, or if the lettering becomes gobbledygook, you're dreaming.

5. Do the same with a digital watch or clock (the one on your microwave, for example). Look at it, look away, and look at it again. According to LaBerge, digital clocks never work properly in dreams.

6. Attempt to alter a detail in the scenery – or make something happen – by willpower. If it changes, you're dreaming.

7. Attempt to push your hand through solid-looking objects. If you can, you're dreaming.

Overcome Rationalizations

Fox and others have noticed how often you come up with ingenious explanations to account for strange dream phenomena while dreaming. So, for example, if you notice someone has two heads, you may say to yourself, "There must be a circus in town." Or if someone's clothes change from moment to moment, you might decide that he or she is modelling clothes for an advertisement – you look around and there is a dream photographer to prove the point!

The key to overcoming such rationalizations is to do a proper dream state test. Any of the ones in the box on page 135 should yield the correct answer.

One thing you should beware of – asking other dream characters whether you're dreaming. They're not reliable sources of information, and will often convince you that you're awake and that you're silly to think otherwise!

Decide This is a Dream

When you decide you are dreaming, suddenly the dream environment will change. Lucid dreaming is the closest thing to "tripping" you will find. Your first task will be to stay cool and not get so excited that you wake up.

I find the best way to do this is to have a prearranged goal for the dream. Once, I decided that when I became lucid I'd travel to see my brother in Chicago (see box, opposite). Other goals you might try are to fly, seek out your ideal dream lover, or change some aspect of the dream environment. I'll give you more ideas in the next chapter.

Lucid Dreaming Space

I believe my dream (see box) gives us a clue to the space we inhabit while lucid dreaming. Like all dream spaces it is constructed by us (hence it is plastic or capable of being moulded) and filled with what we know (by whatever means, including psychic) and what we surmise. This dream clearly contains elements of wish-fulfillment – my brother is aware of me – though this may have been based on his sense of my "presence". It also contains typical dream distortion (curtains into blankets, a

JOE'S DREAM

I became aware I was dreaming and I said I wanted to fly somewhere. I was then aware of flying. I opened one eye and noticed the green grass and trees moving below me. I landed near some narrow railroad tracks. I realized the gauge was too small for Britain and that I was in the United States. Then I remembered my resolution to visit my brother. I let my will pull me there – I kept repeating to myself, "To my brother's place." I felt myself flip out of the top of my head and tumble through darkness, head over heels. Then I was in my brother's bedroom.

He was up and saw me. "Can you see me?" I exclaimed. "Sure," he answered. I hugged him happily. "I can do this all the time now," I said.

I looked through his apartment for evidence of my being there. There were three rooms off a hallway. I went into the first room and a baby started crying. A friend of his and her baby were there. After I hurriedly departed, I said "Did that room have both a blanket and a door on it, or just a blanket?" He said "Both". The other two rooms seemed to have blankets hanging like curtains …

I called my brother that night. He said that at the exact time of my dream, he had been hanging some new curtains he had bought. When I said I had dreamt there was a girl and a baby there, he asked "Barbara?" "Yes," I said. He said he had been thinking of her earlier in the day. I asked if he'd been aware of me in any way at the time. He said it was weird but at some time during the night he had had an awareness of my presence, in the kitchen.

thought into the real presence of the person thought about) showing that my mind fit what it had "picked up" into a dream narrative.

Things to Do While Lucid

Once you become lucid, you'll want to maintain this state as long as possible. The problem is that there is a powerful tendency to lose your self-awareness and be drawn back into the dream environment.

Remaining Lucid

For most people, the first sign a lucid dream is fading is the loss of visual imagery. Re-engaging with the dream world is best accomplished by exercising your dream senses – touch, taste, smell, hearing and especially movement. I usually exercise sight, having decided (following Castenada) to look at my hands whenever I find myself losing lucidity. Stephen LaBerge, who has experimented with many techniques for maintaining lucidity, advocates stretching out your arms and spinning like a top in the dream. It's important to emphasize that you have to actually spin in the dream, not imagine you are spinning. Spinning re-engages your dream senses, especially your kinesthetic sense.

It can also serve to launch you into a new dream location or scenario. While spinning, remind yourself you are dreaming. Think of where you'd like to be when you stop. When you have a sense of having arrived, slow down. If you feel you have awoken – test to be sure.

For me, these techniques of re-engaging your senses supplement the main technique I've used to stay lucid – as soon as I'm lucid I embark on a predetermined task. It's important to decide what you want to do in advance, because otherwise you can have the experience of becoming lucid, and then trying to make up your mind about what to do. First one possibility then another occurs to you. There's so much you could do ... the world's your oyster .. .and before you know it, you've lost your lucid state.

Fun in Lucid Dreams

Just because this is a dream workbook doesn't mean we always have to emphasize work. One of the main reasons to have lucid dreams is that they are great fun. I love flying in lucid dreams. It's certainly a must-do. If you want flying to be more challenging, aim to fly some place in particular. Don't limit yourself to the present – time and everything else is plastic in a lucid dream.

One of the truly great pleasures of lucid dreams is making love. We saw on page 132 how lucid dream sex creates the same bodily response as "real" sex. The difference is that you are not limited in your choice of partners, or by gravity, fitness, body shape or flexibility. Find yourself outside a door to a room. Tell yourself the woman/man/movie star of your dreams is inside and waiting for you. Then enter the room. Sweet dreams!

Altering the Dream Environment

It is worth noting that although the environment of a lucid dream is plastic – moldable by your intentions in the dream – this plasticity has its limits. You can experiment with these limits but when you get into trouble and find yourself faced with a scary situation or dangerous dream adversary, it is much better to alter yourself rather than your environment. (It's also better practice for your waking life – where most of your power lies in changing your perception of the world.)

Paul Tholey has explored various responses to dream adversaries. He feels the most beneficial response is curiosity and that this can be played out by engaging the dream characters in conversation. As soon as you are curious about – rather than scared of – your dream adversary, his or her power is diminished. You are in a much better position to have a conversation of equals.

A good way to start the ball rolling are questions like:

- Who are you?
- Why are you here?
- Why are you acting like this?
- What do I need to know?

Tholey found that his deceased father often appeared to him in his dreams – as a dark figure, full of insults and threats. When Tholey became lucid, he would beat him up. But his sense of triumph was always short-lived, as the dangerous father would appear in another dream. The following dream was the one that made a difference:

I became lucid, while being chased by a tiger, and wanted to flee. I … pulled myself … together, stood my ground, and asked, "Who are you?" The tiger was taken aback but transformed into my father and answered, "I am your father and will now tell you what you are to do!" In contrast to my earlier dreams, I did not attempt to beat him but tried to get involved in a dialogue with him. I told him that he could not order me around. I rejected his threats and insults. On the other hand, I had to admit that some of my father's criticism was justified, and I decided to change my behaviour accordingly. At that moment my father became friendly, and we shook hands. I asked him if he could help me, and he encouraged me to go my own way alone. My father then seemed to slip into my own body, and I remained alone in the dream.

Following this dream, Tholey's father never again appeared as a threatening figure. But more

importantly, Tholey's fear of people in authority in his daily life disappeared. This points to a potential therapeutic application for lucid dreams, which Tholey investigated in a scientific study.

He taught 38 students to have lucid dreams, to approach hostile dream figures with friendly gestures, and to have what Tholey calls a "conciliatory dialogue" with them. He found that if you approached a threatening figure in a courageous manner, looked at him or her openly, and had a conciliatory dialogue, the figure began to shrink and often changed its form.

Integrating the Shadow

Tholey's dream also could be seen as an example of the Jungian notion of integrating the shadow. The shadow tiger becomes his father when challenged, and at the end of the dream, the formerly critical father becomes part of his being.

Stephen LaBerge's approach to dream adversaries is less intellectual and more open-hearted than Tholey's. He emphasizes the power of love and acceptance in relation to threatening dream figures. Below is a self-explanatory example, from his *Lucid Dreaming*:

… Finding myself before two diverging passageways in the castle, I exercised my free will, choosing to take the right-hand one, and shortly came upon a stairway. Curious about where it might lead, I descended the flight of steps and found myself near the top of an enormous subterranean vault. From where I stood at the foot of the stairs, the floor of the cavern sloped steeply down, fading in the distance into darkness. Several hundred yards below I could see what appeared to be a fountain surrounded by marble statuary. The idea of bathing in these symbolically renewing waters captured my fancy, and I proceeded at once down the hillside. Not on foot, however, for whenever I want to get somewhere in my dreams, I fly. As soon as I landed beside the pool, I was at once startled by the discovery that what from above had seemed merely an inanimate statue now appeared unmistakably and ominously alive. Towering above the fountain stood a huge and intimidating genie, the

Guardian of the Spring, as I somehow immediately knew. All my instincts cried out "Flee!" But I remembered that this terrifying sight was only a dream. Emboldened by the thought, I cast aside fear and flew not away, but straight up to the apparition. As is the way of dreams, no sooner was I within reach than we had somehow become of equal size and I was able to look him in the eyes, face to face. Realizing that my fear had created his terrible appearance, I resolved to embrace what I had been eager to reject, and with open arms and heart I took both his hands in mine. As the dream slowly faded, the genie's power seemed to flow into me, and I awoke filled with vibrant energy. I felt like I was ready for anything.

Like in the Tholey example, this dream illustrates the way in which a shadow's power is integrated into his dream being. This had real effects on the way LaBerge met the day.

Learn New Skills

Tholey had a particular interest in applying lucid dreams to sports. In his article, *Applications of Lucid Dreaming in Sports*, he provides many fascinating examples of individuals who learn new skills and master old ones in lucid dreams.

Tholey compares the position of someone in a lucid dream to that of a pilot using a flight simulator. Practicing skills in the virtual world of the dream can lead to an increased capability to handle all kinds of situations. As we're aware from the chapter on scientific discoveries and the earlier section on lucid dreams, your body responds to dream experiences as if they're really happening. This means that educating your body in a dream to do something will make for real improvements in your waking performance. An additional advantage of lucid dream practice is that there is no need to fear injury or being judged harshly by spectators or coaches.

One of Tholey's examples of learning a new skill in a dream was a man who was a black belt in many of the "hard" martial arts – karate, tae kwon do and jujitsu. He had studied these forms and these reflexes were hard-wired into his nervous system. He then attempted to learn a "soft" martial art – aikido. After two years he felt a complete failure. He couldn't overcome the reflexes from his previous training. One night he went to bed after another failure in his training session – he'd been unable to take his attacker to the mat. He was very disheartened.

While falling asleep the situation ran through my mind time and again. While defending myself, the correct balancing movement collided with my inner impulse to execute a hard defensive block, so that I repeatedly ended up unprotected and standing there like a question mark ... a ridiculous and unworthy situation for the wearer of a black belt. During a dream that night, I fell down hard one time instead of rolling away. That day I had made up my mind to ask myself the critical question in this situation: "Am I awake or am I dreaming?" I was immediately lucid. Without thinking very long about it, I immediately went to my Dojo, where I began an unsupervised training session on defense techniques with my dream partner. Time and time again I went through the exercise in a loose and effortless way. It went better every time.

The next evening I went to bed full of expectations. I again achieved a lucid state and practiced aikido further. That's the way it went the whole week until the formal training period started again ... I amazed my instructor with an almost perfect defence. Even though we speeded up the tempo [of our interchanges], I didn't make any serious mistakes. From then on I learned quickly and received my own training licence in one year.

Mastering Old Skills

The same technique can be used by those who already have a skill, but want to improve it. When working with sportsmen who did lucid dream training sessions, Tholey found that he could measure an improvement in motor skills from one dream practice session to another. Slado Solinski is an internationally famous equestrian who uses lucid dreams to improve his performance.

... In a lucid dream I can form my figures to an extremely exact degree – whether in the sand of dressage competition or across the landscape of a cross-country course during military-style competition. I manage to do this in slow motion, giving the horse "assistance" at exactly the right moment in a particular movement phase. During lucid dreaming, "I ride" the course through several times (three to nine times), exactly and completely. Based on this experience, my "body knowledge" is sufficient to get through the course autonomously, i.e. – without and conscious or deliberate effort.

One of the features of Solinski's lucid practice sessions is that he does them in slow motion, something that would be impossible in real life. Tholey points out that the "body knowledge" about which Solinski talks is common to top performers in every sport (and indeed, in many other disciplines). Their movements and responses appear instinctive or unconscious, even when in response to unexpected events. Such automatic responses are not the results of instinct, but of prolonged training and experience.

There is, of course, no reason to limit lucid training sessions to sports. You can practice presentations, performances and interviews.

Spiritual Experience in Lucid Dreams

Finally, I'd like to briefly mention what are often the most profound experiences in lucid dreaming: spiritual or ecstatic experiences. I've never had this kind of transcendent experience in a lucid dream, so I'll leave you with an extract from Stephen LaBerge's *Lucid Dreaming*

Late one summer morning several years ago, I was lying quietly in bed, reviewing the dream I had just awakened from. A vivid image of a road appeared, and by focusing my attention on it, I was able to enter the scene. At this point, I was no longer able to feel my body, from which I concluded I was, in fact, asleep. I found myself driving in my sports car down the dream road, perfectly aware that I was dreaming. I was delighted by the vibrantly beautiful scenery my lucid dream was presenting. After driving a short distance further, I was confronted with a

very attractive, I might say a "dream" of a hitchhiker beside me on the road just ahead. I need hardly say that I felt strongly inclined to stop and pick her up. But I said to myself, "I've had that dream before. How about something new?" So I passed her by, resolving to seek "The Highest" instead. As soon as I opened myself to guidance, my car took off into the air, flying rapidly upward, until it fell behind me like the first stage of a rocket. I continued to fly higher into the clouds, where I passed a cross on a steeple, a star of David, and other religious symbols. As I rose still higher, beyond the clouds, I entered a space that seemed a vast mystical realm: a vast emptiness that was yet full of love; an unbounded space that somehow felt like home. My mood had lifted to corresponding heights, and I began to sing with ecstatic inspiration. The quality of my voice was truly amazing – it spanned the entire range from deepest bass to highest soprano – and I felt as if I were embracing the entire cosmos in the resonance of my voice. As I improvised a melody that seemed more sublime than any I had heard before, the meaning of my song revealed itself and I sang the words, "I praise Thee, O Lord!"

As you might imagine, this dream had a profound effect on LaBerge. It's clearly something he was able to seek after having explored the "earthly" realm of lucid dreams – picking up attractive hitchhikers – and then deciding to seek something higher.

According to Daryl Hewitt, one of LaBerge's students, such ecstatic dreams often have a similar form:

1   A preliminary overcoming of obstacles.
2   An intentional refraining from manipulation of the dream (i.e., not picking up girl).
3   An appeal to the "Higher" (this eclectic formula allows the widest range of dream phenomena).
4   Trust yourself to the flow of the lucid dream.

It's worth noting that transcendent dreams are most likely to develop out of – and in the style of – other spiritual practices. LaBerge has a keen interest in Eastern religions. Ed Kellogg, another proficient lucid dreamer, has had ecstatic lucid dreams based on his work with the Kabbalah. Hewitt has experimented with meditating in lucid dreams. When you become lucid, try to exercise your particular spiritual practice.

9

Psychic Dreaming

Dreaming Through Space and Time

By definition, psychic phenomena don't fit in with our ordinary view of reality. We assume that we know the world through our five senses and that we can know the past and present but not the future. Psychic experiences bring these assumptions into question. This is why they're interesting and challenging.

I can't "explain" many of the dreams that follow. I'm much more interested in exploring what's possible than explaining it.

BASIC CLASSIFICATIONS

Telepathy Becoming aware of something that exists in someone's mind through extra-sensory means. Pure telepathy implies that what you become aware of has no other physical existence – it hasn't been written down. In this case it could also be:

Clairvoyance The perception of objects or events that cannot be perceived by the senses. Pure clairvoyance similarly would imply that no one has seen or knows about the object or event in question, because otherwise it could be telepathy.

Precognition Awareness of something in advance of its occurrence. Pure precognition implies both that no one knows that the event will occur and there is no way of mechanically predicting it.

Filtering

If we move into a house where we can hear any kind of regular noise – trains, church bells, planes – initially the sound can be annoying. But soon we find that we no longer notice it. We have filtered it out. We only become aware of it if a friend visits and says, "What's that?" We then "remember" the regular four o'clock express.

This kind of unconscious filtering goes on all the time. If we didn't do it we would be overwhelmed by the sounds, sights and kinesthetic experiences every time we walked into a shop, down the street or into our workplace.

We clearly don't consciously "decide" what to filter out but it goes on nonetheless and is governed by a number of criteria. A couple of obvious ones are: our interests and concerns – tailors are aware of people's clothes; questions of survival – we won't live long in a city if we ignore traffic; and novelty – we tend to be conscious of what is new.

Another factor that governs our filtering is less obvious. We filter out what doesn't "make sense" or "isn't possible". For example, Floyd Ragsdale (see page 34) had to dream that the problem with the Kevlar machine was in the hoses – he and his supervisor knew that this "wasn't possible".

If you are the sort of person that believes seeing the future or picking up something from someone else's mind is impossible, this filtering process will be very strong in you. Anything that challenges it will be screened out by your day world filters.

However, at night, things are different. We all know that the laws governing time and space are suspended in our dreams. This creates a "space" in which we can have new experiences.

Dream Reality

This has always been the case, particularly in cultures and societies that have been more open to the possibility of psychic phenomena. It is why many of our best-known examples of prophecies – for example, Pharoah's dream of the seven fat cows and the seven thin cows – appeared in dreams.

I'm not going to spend a lot of time talking about famous psychic dreams. As in the rest of the book, my emphasis will be on exploring what you can do to expand your dream awareness and your day world possibilities. I'm going to concentrate on two simple experiments you can do, and which have been tried and tested by myself and others.

Many of the examples in this chapter belong to an earlier period in my life, during which I was very involved in psychic research and an active member of the Society for Psychical Research. My interest in psychic phenomena has continued but it has taken a back seat to working with dream groups and finding ways to reveal the meaning of dreams.

Experimenting with Time

J.W. Dunne's book, *An Experiment With Time*, published in 1927, was the inspiration for one of my first and most successful dream explorations. Dunne was a physicist interested in aeronautics. He was often based abroad and he found himself dreaming of newspaper headlines – from papers that arrived after his dreams. One example:

I seemed to be standing on … the upper slopes of some spur of a hill or mountain. The ground was of a curious white formation. Here and there in this were little fissures, and from these jets of vapour were spouting upward. In my dream I recognized the place as an island of which I had dreamed before – an island which was in imminent peril of a volcano. And when I saw the vapour spouting from the ground, I gasped: "It's the island! Good Lord, the whole thing is going to blow up!" … Forthwith I was seized by the frantic desire to save the four thousand … inhabitants. Obviously there was only one way of doing this, and that was to take them off in ships. There followed the most distressing nightmare, in which I was at a neighbouring island, trying to get the incredulous French authorities to dispatch vessels … All through the dream the number of the people in danger obsessed my mind. I repeated it to everyone I met and at the moment of waking, I was shouting to the "Maire", "Listen! Four thousand people will be killed unless…"

On the next boat, the *Daily Telegraph* arrived. On opening the centre sheet, Dunne found:

VOLCANO DISASTER IN MARTINIQUE

TOWN SWEPT AWAY IN AN AVALANCHE OF FLAME
PROBABLE LOSS OF OVER 40,000 LIVES
BRITISH STEAMER BURNT

One of the most terrible disasters in the annals of the world has befallen the once prosperous town of St Piette, the commercial capital of the French island of Martinique in the West Indies. At eight o'clock on Thursday morning the volcano Mont Pelée which had been quiescent for a century …

Interestingly enough, when Dunne read the headline he read it as 4,000 dead and he told the story in this way for 15 years, until he checked the headline for his book. It was only then he discovered the headline said 40,000.

Later papers showed that the initial figure of 40,000 was inaccurate, and the true figure had nothing in common with the "arrangement of fours and noughts I had both dreamed of and gathered from the first report." This made clear the source for Dunne's dream was the newspaper headline itself.

After a whole series of other such dreams, Dunne realized that "there was nothing unusual in any of these dreams as dreams. They were merely displaced in time." In other words, he would not have been surprised if he'd had the dream *after* reading the paper about it or hearing about it on the radio. What was striking is that it occurred before he had any conscious way to know about it.

Dunne formed the hypothesis that we dream regularly of such future events probably as often as we dream of past events but that we don't become aware of this because:

- We forget most dreams if not immediately, then within a few minutes.
- We don't record them in sufficient detail to be able to recognize coincidences with subsequent events.
- And we don't tend to associate dream occurrences with subsequent events.

The latter, he felt, was the result of an inhibition (or what I would call a filtering process), which kept people from recognizing what was manifestly there. Dunne realized this hypothesis was testable and over the following years he recruited a number of acquaintances to test it out.

On the sixth day of her experiment, one young woman with no previous psychic experience had a dream in which she walked up a path she knew and to her great surprise, found that it ended in a five- or six-barred gate, which had no business to be there. As she reached it, a man and three cows passed on the other side, the man holding out a stick, fishing-rod fashion, over the cows.

The following day, waiting at Plymouth Station for a train, she walked up to one end of a platform and came upon a five- or six-barred gate leading onto the road. As she reached it, a man passed on the other side, driving three brown cows. He was holding a stick and the whole group was arranged just like in the dream.

In another example, Dunne's cousin, who was positive she had never had any kind of psychic experience, dreamed of meeting a German woman in a public park. The woman was dressed in a black skirt with a black-and-white striped blouse and had her hair scraped back.

Two days later she went to stay at a hotel and was told of a person the guests all suspected was German. (This was during WW1.) Shortly afterwards she met this woman in the hotel grounds. The supposed German was dressed in a black skirt with a black-and-white striped blouse and had her hair scraped back in a bun.

Support from Dream Groups

My experience of dream groups provides support for Dunne's hypothesis. As I've shown in my chapter about sharing dreams, psychic coincidences in such groups are not uncommon, even for people who have never previously experienced anything remotely psychic. This is true even for people who have been remembering and recording dreams for some time.

Remembering dreams is not the critical factor. Instead, it is the difficulty of associating dreams with subsequent events. In dream groups, others help you make the connection and can tell you about events or dreams that have occurred in their lives to which you would otherwise have had no access.

My Attempt

I found Dunne's book enormously inspiring and decided to try to emulate his experiment.

I soon found I had a number of successes similar to his subjects. In one of my dreams, the following fragment occurred:

I saw a dog and a teeny dog which changed into two monkeys …

A policeman with a dart gun appeared around the corner of the derelict street, obviously looking for the monkeys. "Here they are!" he shouted running up to the monkeys. The monkeys tried to get away, swinging along the storefront … I shouted to all the people leaning against the storefront to get away, that monkeys scratch when they are frightened.

In a London newspaper two days later I found the following story:

MONKEY BITES TWO BEFORE RECAPTURE

A monkey which esaped from its owner's home in Caledonian Road, Islington, bit a man and a woman in the 30 minutes before it was recaptured. And one of them was offering it a banana.

It was trapped by Mr Donald Johnston an employee of Blue Star Garages.

"I was working in the garage and somebody said they had heard that a monkey was on the loose. I thought this was pretty unlikely in this area but later I was told it had bitten two people so I went to look for it.

"I didn't have to look far because it was on a ledge on a block of flats just across the road. I borrowed a pair of motorbike gloves and went over with some fruit to entice it. When it came down I grabbed the rope tied round its neck and pulled it to the ground. It was petrified.

"Then we put it into the police van. It was screaming and making a lot of noise. The owner came along shortly after and started talking to it and it quietened down and jumped on its owner's shoulder."

This was the only time I have dreamed of a monkey in over 15 years. I certainly wouldn't have recognized the connection between this fragment of a larger dream and the newspaper story had I not consciously looked over my dreams every evening trying to connect them with the day's events. In the dream, I seem to have changed two bites into two monkeys.

While doing a dream workshop in Switzerland I dreamed:

I had got a letter from B & W [an agent to whom I had sent a book manuscript]. I opened it and found two short paragraphs. The first said they thought the book was excellent … The second said they had decided to reject it. I was puzzled by this as I would have expected them to accept a book they thought excellent.

When I arrived home from Switzerland I found a letter from B & W, dated a couple of days after my dream. It was composed of two paragraphs. The first contained the word "excellent", and in the second they accepted (not rejected) the book.

A final small example:

I was reading a story by Jerry in which I became completely involved. I was standing in front of the Town Hall in Kensington High Street.

The following day I was supposed to go to see a movie with my friend Jerry. He called me to arrange where to meet. For some reason, I asked where he was calling from. He replied that he was in the telephone booth in front of the Town Hall in Kensington High Street! (I should add this was nowhere near where he lives and that, as far as I was aware, he had never called from there before.)

Note that none of these dreams are earthshaking nor do the events in them occur undistorted in the dream. As Dunne suggested, "… the majority of such images would not be distinct and separate, but, on the contrary, so blended and intermingled that the components would not be distinguishable as belonging to any special waking event."

An experiment in time

Choose a time when you are not totally immersed in a dull routine. If you're doing exactly the same thing every day, it will be impossible to have a convincing and compelling dream about something unusual.

1 Decide to start the experiment on a particular day. To attune your mind, tell yourself as you fall asleep you are trying to have a dream displaced in time.

2 Record every dream you remember in as much detail as possible. Record both what you perceive and experience in the dream and how you interpret it; if you see a large number of wires and decide in the dream it's a telephone exchange, don't just record "telephone exchange".

3 Every evening, read over your dreams of the two or three previous nights. As you read each one, pretend it has day residue from today. Which of today's events could have sparked the dream images? Can you see any connection between it and the day's events? (This helps you to bypass the resistance to recognizing that you have dreamed something before it happens.) As an example of how difficult it is to catch a connection that is obvious in retrospect, look at my "Troy" dream on page 153.

4 Read a bit of the dream slowly and consider the events of the day. Mark any connections you can see.

5 The final stage is to judge these connections. The chance that a connection is more than "just a coincidence" depends on two factors: how unusual is the individual effect and how often such a coincidence could happen by chance.

In looking over my dream diaries from the period I found about a dozen such Dunneian dreams.

Do try his experiment (see box, left) but don't be too critical in judging your early successes, as belief can open the doors of perception. If a series of minor successes begins to make you believe that you really have psychic abilities, you will find that much more convincing evidence will follow. However, if you insist that each and every coincidence is convincing (where there's room to doubt), your psychic "motor" will never get started.

Psychic Photos

The book *Dream Telepathy*, by Montague Ullman, Stanley Krippner and Alan Vaughan presents powerful scientific evidence for dream telepathy. In a series of experiments, they showed that a dreamer could pick up images from photographs that were

DREAM TELEPATHY

The Dream Telepathy team tried many innovative experiments to map the limits of dream telepathy. In one, the Grateful Dead (a popular acid-rock group) agreed to host an experiment during a series of six concerts held 45 miles away from the laboratory.

Each concert was attended by about 2,000 young people many of whom, observers noted, were in an "altered state of consciousness". During each concert a randomly chosen image was flashed up on a big screen and the audience was asked to "Try and use your ESP to 'send' this picture to Malcolm Bessent … He is now in the Maimonides Dream Laboratory in Brooklyn." In one experiment, the audience were asked to transmit this picture of the Seven Spinal Chakras by M.K. Scralian. (A chakra is an energy centre in the body according to Eastern philosophy.)

being "transmitted" by a sender in another room (see box below). Their experiment is easy to recreate. Find a friend who is interested and ask him or her to choose a very unusual or striking image. Suggest he or she concentrates on the image and, on an agreed evening, thinks of you.

Before you go to sleep, say to yourself, "I'll have and remember a dream that will contain the image that [friend's name] is concentrating on." Make this into a mantra and keep repeating it as you go to sleep. Picture yourself comparing your dream with the photo and being delighted by the similarity. Then write down all your dreams in as much detail as possible.

When I was the sender, I'd concentrate on the image for about 10 minutes on the agreed date. Dunne's time displacement clearly applied in such experiments. My receivers (often a class I was

teaching) might receive the photo that night, or the nights before or after I chose the photo. For this reason, you need to allow your friend at least a week in which to have his or her dream.

When checking your results have the target image physically in front of you. (Don't let your friend describe it on the phone.) Examine the image closely and compare it to your dream accounts, even if at first glance you think you have missed the target entirely. Look at shapes, themes, clothes, etc.

Malcolm Bessent dreamed:

I was very interested in ... using natural energy ... I was talking to this guy who said he'd invented a way of using solar energy and he showed me this box ... to catch the light from the sun which was all we needed to generate and store the energy ... I was discussing with this other guy a number of other areas of communication and we were exchanging ideas on the whole thing ... He was suspended in mid air or something ... I was thinking about rocket ships ... I'm remembering a dream I had ... about an energy box and ... a spinal cord.

A very striking hit! These experiments show that physical distance is no bar to dream telepathy. However, a comparison with other experiments showed that there was no increase in the success rate when there were many senders rather than just one. So you don't need 2,000 people to insure a successful telepathy experiment ...

Dream Dialogue

As I've already shown in Sharing Dreams (see pages 112–27), when people regularly share dreams, a psychic link can develop between them. Here I'll give details of a sustained series of psychic dreams I had over a two-year period with Pete, one of my students who became a friend.

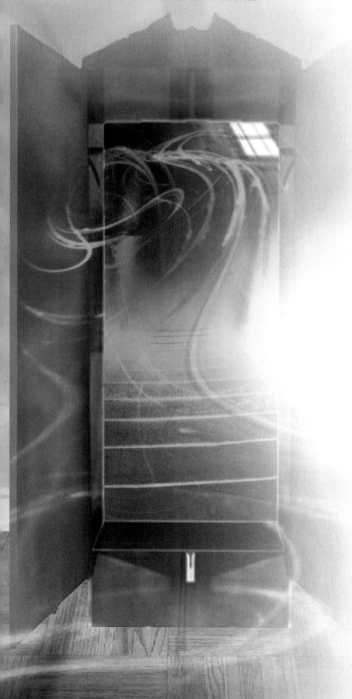

Pete enrolled in one at my adult education parapsychology classes. He had been interested in the occult and ESP for some time. He was also very interested in his dream life, often remembering and recording several dreams a night. After I spoke in one of the classes about telepathic and precognitive dreams, Pete came up to me and said that, though he'd been writing down his dreams for some time, he'd never had one that he considered to be precognitive. I told him confidently he'd have such a dream the following week. I had a sense that saying this would open the door to such a dream.

The following week Pete approached me before the class and told me that he'd failed. He'd remembered and recorded 13 dreams, but none of them had proved to be precognitive. I asked him to choose one dream to tell me. After looking through his dream diary, he selected the following dream:

The brat next door comes into my room. I am very hospitable and feed him, but he acts boorishly as if he owns the place. He opens the wardrobe and to my amazement there is another door in the back of the wardrobe, which leads into the attic next door …

I told Pete he'd just had his first "precognitive" dream. I was just about to lead a guided fantasy with the class. It had an induction in which they would open the door to a wardrobe in their rooms and discover another door at the back, which opened magically for them. (Strictly speaking, of course, this dream wasn't precognitive, as I knew I was going to be doing this exercise.)

Like many of the dreams that followed, this dream involved a kind of psychic "selection." Pete could have chosen any of his 13 dreams to tell me, but a sixth sense led him to pick the one that contained the psychic content. As the dream series continued to develop, this awareness became more explicit, and both of us developed dream "tracers".

A year later, Pete joined a dream group I was leading. Most of the more than 20 psychic dreams we had together occurred over the next six months. These dreams were equally distributed between the two of us, and involved a variety of different "psychic" contents.

An example of how an awareness of a psychic connection was developing was a night in which I dreamed of visiting a friend in Collier's Wood, an area in south London, while Pete dreamed of:

a picnic in a forest … people in orange clothes … they are either walkers or miners … There are stones and stone circles … I stand in one circle and am aware that this is a place of power. I … wonder if I am emitting psychic power.

A miners' forest = Collier's Wood. In this dream, Pete had an explicit awareness that something psychic was happening.

On some nights, Pete and I would "schedule" having a common dream. On one such occasion, at three in the morning, Pete had a dream in which a lizard was being attacked by an insect around its neck. At almost exactly the same time I dreamed about dinosaurs.

There were several huge eggs that were cracking. When one was cracking this guy called over a lady expert but by the time she had identified the eggs the dinosaur was out and growing at a extraordinary pace. I told the guy to grab and kill it. He grabbed it, but the dinosaur pecked viciously at him and he let go, surprised and hurt. I grabbed a dinosaur and another guy hacked at its neck with a butter knife.

So, having agreed to have a common dream, we both dreamed of lizards (in my case, a very large lizard) and of the lizards being attacked on the neck.

On several of the occasions in which I had a common dream with Pete, there would be other elements of the dream that coincided with other members of the dream group. It's almost as if we can tune into a psychic "space" in a dream, and this enables us to link up with a number of people.

Some of the shared dreams we had involved events in the other's life, of which there was no way we could have been aware. One night I dreamed I was listening to some music in the park. While I was doing so,

a boy started to remove my bike. I rushed over to him and started pushing him around, really enjoying myself, saying, "What are you doing with my bike?" While I was doing this, the boy's father came and got on my bike and started to ride off with it. I realized I had allowed myself to get carried away …

It turned out that the evening before I dreamed this, Pete had left his bike outside a friend's house. While he was inside, his rear light was stolen, for the second time in this location. On the way home, Pete fell to daydreaming of leaving his bike outside the house and hiding, waiting for the thief to come. He then caught the thief and gave him a good beating. His daydream continued with the boy's father coming to his friend's house and asking for the person who owned a bicycle …

My dream mixed up the reality – Pete's rear light being stolen – and his daydream.

Informal Experiments

Pete and I did several informal experiments. Once, while I was in Chicago, I bought a postcard of Peter Blume's "The Rock", a surreal painting of a number of people worshipping a rock in a vividly-coloured Dali-esque landscape. I thought it would be a good "target" and sent it to Pete. I wrote on the back, "Dear Pete. This card was your precog target for last night – did you dream about it?" In fact, Pete's

dream the night before he received the card did have a resemblance to it. He dreamed:

At Joe's, seeing him for the first time after the break. He tells me of some sci-fi film – did I see it? I didn't but it seems Roy [a mutual friend] did. They talk about it. Joe then mentions a series of sci-fi fantasy films, but I have seen none of them.

The science fiction or fantasy theme does correspond with the card I'd chosen. In the dream Pete seems to be aware of the psychic connection (he's seeing me for the first time since the break) though the dream rather makes a joke of it – he hasn't seen any of the films I mention.

This dream does seem to be genuinely precognitive. Though obviously I knew I had sent him the card, I had no idea on which day it would arrive at his door in the UK.

On another occasion, Pete tuned into an experiment I was doing with one of my classes. I had asked them all to have a dream about a photo I would be thinking about on a particular night. The photograph showed a Chinese dance troupe, which included a number of people wearing wings. Pete dreamed:

In a street I come unexpectedly upon Jeff [a friend] – he looks absolutely amazing, dressed in a yellow safari suit … with a butterfly net in one hand, stalking butterflies. There are many brightly coloured butterflies, large furry ones, yellow ones and amidst them all is one which is very special.

The dancers in the photograph did indeed look like brightly coloured butterflies.

Dream Interventions

One of the most striking dreams in this series was a dream in where I actively intervened in Pete's dream to change it, an intervention which Pete experienced. My dream:

Pete has decided to commit suicide. He has bought an old Junker which he plans to drive into the sea and kill himself … Pete then seems to be in the sea. I physically struggle with him, and eventually he decides not to drown himself. I then tell him I had a precognitive dream in which he tried to commit suicide.

When I next saw Pete I was keen to check out this dream, since it had such a clear tracer in it (I tell him I had a precognitive dream). Pete told me he'd had three or four really bad nights where he'd been having unpleasant, anxiety-filled dreams, so much so that he'd wanted to avoid deep sleep. The night I had my dream, he had the sense that every time he got into "deep water", so to speak, I was pulling him out. After this, his series of anxiety-filled nights ended. What I believe is unprecedented in these dreams is the way both of us seem to be aware I am making a real intervention in his dreams – while we're dreaming.

In another, similar dream, in which Pete was the "active" partner, he had a dream in which he became lucid. He was on a bus that was out of control – he became lucid and then stopped it, then "projected" himself through the window. The same night I dreamed I was on a tram going down a hill. I didn't know how to stop it and was having "a hell of a time" though eventually I did manage to bring it to a standstill.

I hope this short taster is sufficient to inspire you to experiment with trying to develop a psychic link with a dream partner. It's fascinating and enormously satisfying to experience such a link developing.

PREDICTING THE DERBY

Pete regularly worked in a betting shop and one year dared me to predict the winner of the Derby in a dream. I told him, "No problem. I'll have the dream the night before the race."

Four nights before the race I dreamed about a dream group. Stanley Krippner (a famous dream parapsychologist and co-author of *Dream Telepathy*) was in the dream and fell in love with a woman … The next part of the dream involved an army which was being attacked near Wolverhampton or Birmingham. The enemy was luring the soldiers out of their base. The English soldiers were so undisciplined they ran out of the base to chase them, and then were surrounded.

The last bit of the dream immediately reminded me of the Trojan horse, and I wrote this down in my notes. I told the dream and my associations to the dream group of which Pete was a member. Neither of us realized it was the dream we were looking for.

As I didn't have a dream the night before the Derby, I didn't bother to look at the runners in the morning. (I had not a clue about horses or who would run.) So I didn't notice that a horse called "Troy" was running. Of course, Troy won the race.

Afterwards, we kicked ourselves. This was obviously the dream we were looking for – it had my usual tracer in it – a famous parapsychologist (and a dream one to boot!), it had a reference to Pete – he was from Wolverhampton, and it had a clear association to a horse that Pete knew was running in the race.

This just shows how hard it can be to make a connection between a dream and a real-life event, even when it is signposted in symbolic neon letters.

Afterword

I hope you've enjoyed this book and that it's inspired you to start recording your dreams and working with them. Even if it has, I suspect you haven't given all the techniques in the book a fair chance.

Try to experiment with a new way of exploring your dreams regularly – say once a month. The advantage of this is that each exercise will bring out a different aspect of what your dreams are saying and will give you new insights from them.

This book can only be the merest introduction to dream work. I hope I've piqued your curiosity enough to go to some of its original sources. You'll find them to be deep wells of inspiration. Some of the recommended authors have fearsome reputations – yet their books are often surprisingly readable. For example, Freud's Interpretation of Dreams won a prize for literature.

It was part of the basic Greek practice to share your dream accomplishments with others. "Testifying" in this way can lead to further successful dream work. I, for one, would be happy to hear about them. Feel free to email me at: solutiondreams@googlemail.com

Please note I won't be able to enter into an extended correspondence on this or any other matter concerning dream meaning.

Working with others is one of the best ways to develop your dream skills. There may well be dream workshops or courses near you. If you're interested in my dream groups or workshops, check out what's on offer at: www.solutiondreams.com

Index

A

Amplification 58

Associations 93–4

B

Barrett, Deirdre, 34

Berry, Patricia 61

Boss, Medard 65–7

Brain activity during sleep 24

C

Cartwright, Rosalind, 37, 104, 105

Chemicals and dreaming 28

Choices in dreams 85–6

Collective unconscious, the 55–6

Compensation 54

Composite figures 49

"Condensation" 49

Conflicts in dreams 86

Creativity and dreaming 28, 33

Crisis dreaming 105

D

"Day residue" 48

Displacement 51

Domhoff, G.W. 71

Dream appreciation 124

Dream characters 61–2, 85

Dream, clarifying the 85–8

Dream coincidences 121–3

Dream conservation 62

Dream deprivation 26

Dream dialogue 150–53

Dream diary, keeping a 15, 16–17

Dream dimensions 105

Dream group

finding a 126

language 119

phenomenon 119–23

types of 126–7

Dream incubation 32–3

Dream interpretation 48, 49, 51, 77–8, 82–8

Dream interventions 153

Dream language 53, 89–92

Dream location, significance of 85

Dream partner, finding a 125

Dream paralysis 27

Dream recall 12, 13, 25–6

categories of 18

improving 18–19

respect for the 77

Dream senses, improving 20–21

Dream settings 96

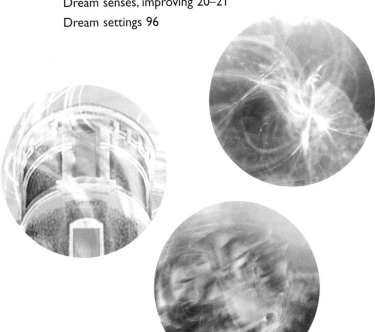

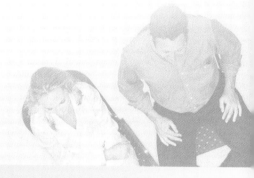

Further Reading

Solution Dreams
Deirdre Barrett, Ph.D., *The Committee of Sleep: How Artists, Scientists and Athletes Use Dreams for Creative Problem-Solving, and How You Can Too.* Crown Publishers, 2001.

What We Can Learn From ...
Freud
Sigmund Freud, *The Interpretation of Dreams.* Penguin Books, 1991.

Jung
Carl Jung, *Memories, Dreams and Reflections.* Fontana, 1995.

Maggie Hyde and Michael McGuinness (illustrator), *Introducing Jung.* Icon Books Ltd, 2004.

Hillman and Berry
James Hillman, *Dreams and the Underworld.* Harper Paperbacks, 1979.

Patricia Berry, "An Approach to Dreaming," *Spring: An Annual of Archetypal Psychology and Jungian Thought. XXV:2, 58-79.*

Boss
Medard Boss, *I Dreamt Last Night.* John Wiley & Sons, 1978.

Medard Boss, *The Analysis of Dreams.* Philosophical Library, 1958.

Dream Work
G. W. Domhoff, "A New Neurocognitive Theory of Dreams." *Dreaming,* 11, 13-33, 2001.

Rosalind Cartwright, Ph.D. and Lynne Lamberg, *Crisis Dreaming: Using Your Dreams to Solve Problems*. Harper Perennial, 1993.

Strephon Kaplan Williams, *The Jungian-Senoi Dreamwork Manual*. Journey Press, 1980.

Sharing Dreams

Montague Ullman, M.D. and Nan Zimmerman, *Working with Dreams: Self-Understanding, Problem-Solving and Enriched Creativity through Dream Appreciation*. Crucible, 1979.

Jeremy Taylor, *Where People Fly and Water Runs Uphill*. Warner Books, Inc., 1992.

Lucid Dreams

Stephen LaBerge, *Lucid Dreaming*. Ballantine Books, 1998.

Stephen LaBerge & Howard Rheingold, *Exploring the World of Lucid Dreams*. Ballantine Books, 1990.

Tholey, Paul "A Model of Lucidity Training as a Means of Self-Healing and Psychological Growth," in *Conscious Mind, Sleeping Body*, eds. J. Gackenbach and S. LaBerge, Plenum Publishers, 1988.

Tholey, Paul, "Applications of Lucid Dreaming in Sports." www.spiritwatch.ca/applications_of_lucid_dreaming

Hewitt, Daryl "Induction of Ecstatic Lucid Dreams." www.spiritwatch.ca/inductio

Dreaming Through Time and Space

Montague Ullman, Stanley Krippner, Alan Vaughan, *Dream Telepathy: Experiments in Nocturnal Extra-Sensory Perception*. Hampton Roads Publishing Company, 2003.

J. W. Dunne, *An Experiment With Time*. Hampton Roads Publishing Company, 2001.

2 ACKNOWLEDGMENTS

Acknowledgments

Like every author, I owe a huge debt to all those dream explorers who came before me and without whom this book would have been impossible. I'm especially grateful to all those who have shared dreams with me, especially those who have allowed their dreams to be included here.

My readers – John Fraser and Sam Kolupov – have removed bad grammar, poor punctuation and confused expressions from this book. Maggie Hyde helped enormously with the chapter on Jung. Julie Barber acted as my editor – her help has been completely invaluable.

I have made every effort to trace the copyright holders of material quoted in this book. I am grateful to the following authors and publishers who have given me permission to quote from or refer to their texts:
The Sigmund Freud Estate: Sigmund Freud, *Interpretation of Dreams* (Penguin Books, 1991).
Deirdre Barrett, Ph.D., *The Committee of Sleep: How Artists, Scientists and Athletes Use Dreams for Creative Problem-Solving, and How You Can Too* (Crown Publishers, 2001).
Montague Ullman, M.D. and Nan Zimmerman, *Working with Dreams: Self Understanding, Problem Solving and Enriching Creativity Through Dream Appreciation* (Crucible, 1979).
Jeremy Taylor, *Where People Fly and Water Runs Uphill* (Warner Books, Inc., 1992).
Rosalind Cartwright, Ph.D. and Lynne Lamberg, *Crisis Dreaming: Using Your Dreams to Solve Problems* (Harper Perennial, 1993).
Chris Salewicz, *McCartney* (St Martin's Press, 1986).
Hampton Roads Publishing Company: Montague Ullman, Stanley Krippner, Alan Vaughan, *Dream Telepathy: Experiments in Nocturnal Extra-Sensory Perception* (Hampton Roads Publishing Company, 2003).
J.M. Dunne, *An Experiment in Time* (Hampton Roads Publishing Company, 2001).
Stephen LaBerge: *Lucid Dreaming* (Ballantine Books, 1998).
Stephen LaBerge and Howard Rheingold, *Exploring the World of Lucid Dreams* (Ballantine Books, 1990).
Strephon Kaplan Williams, *The Jungian-Senoi Dreamwork Manual* (Journey Press, 1980).

Picture Credits
page 24 Allan Hobson /SPL; page 26 (b) Professor Stuart Campbell; page 35 Plainpicture/Photolibrary; pages 44, 47 Mary Evans/Sigmund Freud Copyrights; pages 45 (l), 53 Mary Evans Picture Library; pages 45 (r), 65 Hulton-Deutsch Collection/Corbis; page 52 Getty Images; page 58 Alen MacWeeney/Corbis; page 64 Getty Images; page 78 Ted Tamburo/Photolibrary